United States Presidents

John F. Kennedy

Series Consultant:
Don M. Coerver, professor of history
Texas Christian University, Fort Worth, Texas

Karen Bornemann Spies

Enslow Publishers, Inc.

40 Industrial Road	PO Box 38
Box 398	Aldershot
Berkeley Heights, NJ 07922	Hants GU12 6BP
USA	UK

http://www.enslow.com

Library of Congress Cataloging-in-Publication Data

Spies, Karen Bornemann.
    John F. Kennedy / Karen Bornemann Spies.
       p. cm. — (United States presidents)
    Includes bibliographical references (p. 145) and index.
    Summary: Examines the military service, family life, political
career, assassination, and legacy of the thirty-fifth president of
the United States.
    ISBN 0-7660-1039-2
    1. Kennedy, John F. (John Fitzgerald), 1917–1963—Juvenile
literature. 2. Presidents—United States—Biography—Juvenile
literature. [1. Kennedy, John F. (John Fitzgerald), 1917–1963.
2. Presidents.] I. Title. II. Series.
E842.Z9S68   1999
973.922'092—dc21
[B]   98-29553
                                   CIP
                                   AC

Printed in the United States of America

10 9 8 7 6 5 4 3

To Our Readers:
All Internet Addresses in this book were active and appropriate when we
went to press. Any comments or suggestions can be sent by e-mail to
Comments@enslow.com or to the address on the back cover.

Illustration Credits: Henrietta Oppenheim, p. 69; John F.
Kennedy Library, pp. 4, 13, 17, 19, 23, 27, 35, 44, 48, 54, 60, 63, 84,
85, 86, 87, 90, 102, 110, 118, 122; Library of Congress, pp. 33, 75,
80, 125; Lyndon Baines Johnson Library, p. 99; National Archives
and Records Administration, p. 124, 127; National Archives and
Records Administration, Warren Commission, p. 129; Reproduced
by Enslow Publishers, Inc., p. 8.

Source Document Credits: John F. Kennedy Library, p. 20–21,
29, 73, 141; National Archives and Records Administration, p. 133.

Cover Illustration: John F. Kennedy Library.

Contents

The Kennedys arrive in Dallas on November 22, 1963, looking fit and happy. Little did they suspect the tragic events the day would bring.

1

DISASTER IN DALLAS

I magine that today is November 22, 1963. The thirty-fifth president of the United States, John F. Kennedy, and his wife, Jacqueline, are arriving in Dallas, Texas. The president is scheduled to give a speech at the Dallas Trade Mart.

At Love Field, the Dallas airport, about four thousand people are waiting. They are hoping for a glimpse of the handsome forty-six-year-old president and his glamorous thirty-four-year-old wife, popularly known as Jackie. The president and Mrs. Kennedy smile as they step out of *Air Force One*, the presidential jet. In a moment, the crowd senses the Kennedy charisma. The youthful president looks tanned and fit. Jackie, already famous for setting fashion trends, looks radiant in a stylish pink suit with a matching pillbox hat.

Texas governor John Connally and his wife, Nellie, are on hand to greet the first couple. Vice-President Lyndon B.

Johnson and his wife, Lady Bird, also Texans, are there, too, and step forward to shake the Kennedys' hands. Connally and Johnson have invited the president to tour their state, hoping to put an end to rumors that liberal and conservative Democratic party politicians in Texas are feuding and splitting the party's support. Liberal politicians traditionally create new programs as they make public policy, whereas conservatives tend to resist political change. Texas senator Ralph Yarborough is a liberal; however, Governor Connally is more conservative. Vice-President Johnson is a close friend of Connally's, but he holds many liberal political views that are similar to Yarborough's. President Kennedy hopes that Johnson will be able to help Connally and Yarborough get along. Party unity is vital since the following year, 1964, is an election year. This trip is also a good opportunity for the president to get more exposure to southern voters.

Prior to the trip, Kennedy's advisers feared that the crowds coming out to see the president might be unfriendly. From 1961 to 1962 alone, thirty-four death threats were reported against Kennedy from the state of Texas.[1] In the 1960 presidential election, which Kennedy won by only a slim margin, the majority of voters in Dallas had supported Republican Richard M. Nixon. Although they were traditionally Democrats, these Texas voters had supported Nixon rather than vote for Kennedy, whose support of civil rights issues was unpopular there. Kennedy had worked hard to ensure that African Americans would be guaranteed the right to vote and would have equal opportunities for jobs. However, traditionally, southerners opposed equal rights for African Americans. In addition, some groups in the Dallas area were critical of the president for not dealing more forcefully with the Communist nations of Cuba and the Soviet Union (USSR).

So the friendly Dallas welcome is a pleasant surprise to the president. He comments to Baxton Bryant, a Dallas minister, "This doesn't look like an anti-Kennedy crowd."[2]

A motorcade, or procession of cars, forms for the trip from the airport into the city of Dallas. The Kennedys sit in the backseat of their limousine. In the same limo, Governor and Mrs. Connally sit in front of the Kennedys on small jump seats. The first two cars in the motorcade are filled with Dallas police officers and agents of the Secret Service, the federal agency assigned to protect the president and his family. The president's car is third. The rest of the motorcade includes cars carrying Vice-President and Mrs. Johnson, congressmen, local leaders, and White House staffers. A press car carries reporters from the national news agencies.

By 11:45 A.M., the motorcade is following its planned route to the Dallas Trade Mart, where the president will speak to Dallas business leaders, describing his support for business development throughout the nation. He also plans to talk about America's role as a leader in keeping world peace. The route of the motorcade has been published in advance by Kennedy's own staff, who hope to encourage as many people as possible to come out and see him. The prospect of large crowds, however, makes security more difficult.

The president's limousine is equipped with a removable plastic bubble top. It offers protection from bad weather, and because it is designed to deflect bullets, it keeps the president safe from potentially threatening

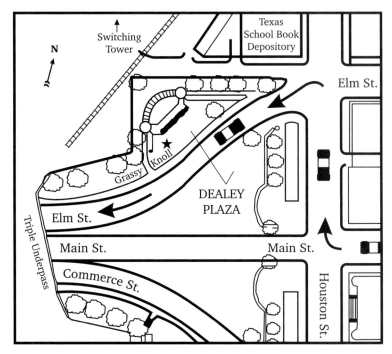

The proposed route of the presidential motorcade through downtown Dallas was published in advance, so that crowds would be encouraged to come out.

situations. The Secret Service wants to use the bubble for increased security. However, Kennedy prefers to ride in an open car, because he wants spectators to see him better. The president seems unconcerned about security. Just that morning, he told his wife, "If someone wanted to shoot me from a window with a rifle, nobody can stop it. So why worry about it?"[3]

Friendly spectators line the motorcade's route into Dallas. One little girl holds up a sign that reads, "Mr. President, will you please stop and shake hands with me?"[4] When he sees the sign, the president stops the motorcade to grant her request.

About two hundred thousand people line the motorcade route. The crowds are thickest in downtown Dallas where the motorcade turns onto Main Street, approaching Dealey Plaza, a town square. At the corner of Main and Houston streets, the cars make a ninety-degree right turn. They head north to where the Texas School Book Depository building overlooks Dealey Plaza. Mrs. Connally turns and says, "You sure can't say Dallas doesn't love you, Mr. President."[5]

The time is 12:30 P.M. Suddenly it sounds like a firecracker has exploded. Then there are more sounds—gunshots! People dive for cover. No one knows for sure the source of the shots.

Someone in the president's car screams out, "Oh no, no, no!"[6] Kennedy slumps toward his wife, splattering her perfect pink suit with red blood. Governor Connally is also seriously wounded. Jackie Kennedy jumps up from her seat and seems to scramble onto the back of the car, frantically looking for help. Secret Service agent Clint Hill is riding in the car behind the Kennedys. He jumps off his slow-moving vehicle and dives onto the presidential limousine. After Agent Hill makes sure Jackie gets back in her seat, she huddles over her husband, trying to protect him as well as herself from any more sniper's bullets.

Quickly, the president's driver, Secret Service agent Bill Greer, pulls out of the motorcade. He races toward Parkland Hospital, about four miles away. Jackie gently cradles her husband's head in her lap. At first, no one knows how severe the president's injuries are.

Merriman Smith, a United Press International (UPI) reporter, is riding in the front seat of the news reporters' car. He grabs the car radio-telephone and calls his office.

At 12:34 P.M., his news bulletin is transmitted around the world: "THREE SHOTS WERE FIRED AT PRESIDENT KENNEDY'S MOTORCADE TODAY IN DOWNTOWN DALLAS."[7] Locally, all sorts of false rumors are spreading. One is that Vice-President Johnson is shot or has suffered a heart attack.

At the Parkland Hospital emergency room, doctors work feverishly on the severely injured president. His wife insists on remaining in the emergency room. The president's head wounds are so massive that the doctors are unable to save him. A priest administers extreme unction. In the Catholic faith, this ceremony is performed when a person is about to die. The priest prays for forgiveness of the dying person's sins. The doctors then declare the president dead. Mrs. Kennedy bends and kisses her slain husband and places one of her rings on his finger.

Governor Connally undergoes surgery in another emergency room. He has suffered bullet wounds to the back, chest, wrist, and thigh. After several hours, the nation learns that Connally will recover.

Walter Cronkite of CBS News in New York is shocked when he receives the UPI news bulletin that the nation's young president has been assassinated. CBS interrupts its broadcasting of the soap opera *As the World Turns* to have Cronkite announce the tragic news to the nation. The world is stunned into disbelief. Almost everyone alive at the time will remember exactly where they were and what they were doing when they heard the news of John F. Kennedy's death. Even those who had not voted for President Kennedy felt a sense of personal loss.[8]

John F. Kennedy's memory lives on today. His life is remembered as a time of hope for America.

2

GROWING UP A KENNEDY

John Fitzgerald Kennedy was descended from Irish immigrants, the Fitzgeralds and the Kennedys. His ancestors had come to Boston, Massachusetts, from Ireland to escape the terrible potato famines of the 1840s. They may have started out penniless, but both the Fitzgeralds and the Kennedys were determined to succeed in their new land.

Patrick Joseph "P. J." Kennedy, John F. Kennedy's father's father, left school at age fourteen. He saved his money and bought two saloons. As his saloons became more profitable, he also invested in a liquor-importing business. The success of his ventures earned him the reputation as a trustworthy businessman and a good listener. These qualities made him a natural for politics. He was soon elected to leadership positions in the Democratic party. Eventually, P. J. served in both the Massachusetts state legislature and the state senate.

John Fitzgerald Kennedy was named after his mother's father, John Francis Fitzgerald. Fitzgerald, commonly known as "Honey Fitz," served in the state senate and the United States Congress. He also became one of Boston's most popular mayors.

The beginning of one of America's strongest political dynasties was forged when Rose Fitzgerald, Honey Fitz's oldest daughter, fell in love with Joseph (Joe) Kennedy, P. J.'s oldest son. Honey Fitz had his doubts that strong-willed, hard-driving Joe Kennedy would be the best match for his favorite child.[1] Nevertheless, the couple continued to see each other. Joe graduated from Harvard University in 1912 and went into banking. He was determined to be involved in activities that would build him a position of wealth and power. In January 1914, at the age of twenty-five, he became one of the youngest bank presidents in the United States. Finally, after Joe attained success as a bank president, Honey Fitz agreed that Joe and Rose could marry. Their wedding took place on October 7, 1914.

Joe and Rose Kennedy purchased a small house in Brookline, Massachusetts. A year after the wedding, Rose and Joe's first child, Joseph, Jr., was born. Their second child, John Fitzgerald, or Jack, as they called him, was born on May 29, 1917.

At the time, the United States was already involved in World War I. Joseph Kennedy became assistant general manager at Bethlehem Steel's Fore River shipyard in Quincy, Massachusetts, where United States Navy ships were built. The job allowed him to be involved in the war effort without actually having to serve in the military.

As World War I drew to a close, Joe began to develop a new business talent—investing in the stock market. He

Joe Kennedy, Sr., holds Joe, Jr. (left), and little John (right).

soon earned a reputation as a sharp trader. By the middle of the 1920s, Joseph Kennedy's fortune was estimated at about $2 million.[2]

The more successful Joseph Kennedy became at business, the more time he spent away from home. Rose missed the active social life she had enjoyed before her marriage. After the birth of daughter Rosemary in 1918, Rose was busy with three children under the age of five.

In February 1920, she had just given birth to the fourth Kennedy child, Kathleen, when scarlet fever attacked little Jack. This disease was highly contagious and almost killed the boy, who was not yet three years old. He spent nearly three months in the hospital. During his recovery, the boy already showed the type of social charm that would serve him so well later in life. The nurses loved his wide, easy smile and his willingness to converse. Jack's illness had one positive result. It jolted his father away from his preoccupation with work. Thereafter, for the rest of his life, Joseph Kennedy remained deeply involved in his children's affairs.

Three more children soon arrived in the Kennedy family. Eunice was born in 1921, Patricia in 1924, and Robert in 1925.

Little by little, Rose Kennedy became increasingly focused on the family's Catholic religion. In the Catholic faith, the pope is the head of the Church. He and other high Church officials set the rules of conduct. Instruction in the faith and regular attendance at church services, called mass, are expected. As a good Catholic, Rose insisted that her children attend church regularly.

With seven children, Rose had to be organized. Although she employed a housekeeper, a cook, and governesses for the children, Rose maintained strict control over the household. She regularly walked about the house with notes pinned to her dress reminding her of the day's most important tasks. Meals occurred at set times. If a child was late, he or she would not be allowed to eat any of the food that had already been served. Topics were preset for mealtime discussions. Usually they related to Church holidays or current events.

Joseph Kennedy stressed to the children the importance of obeying and respecting their mother. He also emphasized the need for them to succeed in sports, business, education, or whatever venture one might attempt. He repeatedly told his children, "We don't want any losers around here. In this family we want winners."[3]

Jack favored his father. His mother did not understand his playful nature, and she disliked his sloppiness. His shirt was rarely tucked in, and his collar usually stood up. He was often late to meals, but the cook took pity on him and fed him later in the kitchen. Jack deliberately made it a point to set his own course rather than fit into the mold his mother expected him to assume.[4] Still, he seemed to yearn for more positive attention from her. Jack cried whenever she packed her bags to go away on a trip. When he was five, Rose left for a three-week trip to California with her sister. Jack said sarcastically, "Gee, you're a great mother to go away and leave your children alone."[5] Between 1929 and 1934, Rose Kennedy took seventeen trips to Europe by herself to purchase the latest fashions.[6]

Some of the best times Jack and his mother spent together were during his frequent childhood illnesses. He had whooping cough, bronchitis, and asthma. Because he was born with one leg shorter than the other, his back was out of position. As a result, Jack suffered from frequent backaches. To distract him from the pain, Rose read to Jack every day for an hour or two. His favorite tales included *Peter Pan, Sinbad the Sailor, Treasure Island,* and stories about King Arthur and his knights of the Round Table. History and biography would continue to fascinate Jack all his life. His interest in reading set him apart from his brothers and sisters. It was one way Jack could excel over his older brother, Joe, Jr.

There was no doubt that Jack's parents favored Joe, Jr. As the oldest son, young Joe was expected to take a leadership role. His strong, commanding temperament naturally led him to take charge. He was neat and orderly, qualities his mother particularly appreciated. His parents expected him to help the younger children learn sports and do their homework.

Jack could not seem to resist competing with his older brother. The two had many fistfights. Once Joe, Jr., challenged Jack to race their bikes around the block, each going in the opposite direction. Eventually, they crashed together at the finish line, sending Jack to the hospital for twenty-eight stitches on several parts of his body. Even though Jack lost most battles to Joe, Jr., he never stopped trying to win.

Jack began his education at the Devotion School, a public elementary school named after Edward Devotion, an early benefactor of Brookline, Massachusetts. In the fall of 1924, when he was seven, his father transferred him to the Dexter School. It was a private country day school attended by the sons of wealthy Boston families.

In 1926, Joseph Kennedy began yet another business venture when he purchased Film Booking Offices (FBO).

Jack Kennedy at age five.

He quickly earned a reputation as a clever, bold Hollywood producer. He also earned a reputation for carrying on romantic relationships with Hollywood starlets.[7] Perhaps he set a poor example for his sons, who later followed their father's pattern of seeking glamorous romances outside his marriage.

His financial success earned Joseph Kennedy respect in both Hollywood and New York, but not in Boston. Old families of wealth or power refused to acknowledge newcomers to Boston's financial and social circles. Nor were Irish Catholics like Joe Kennedy accepted into Boston's most prestigious social clubs. In 1927, Joe Kennedy decided to move to New York City. He rented a home in Riverdale, on the Hudson River north of the city. Jack attended grades four through six at Riverdale Country Day School.

Soon after the move to New York, Joseph Kennedy purchased a large home in Hyannis Port, Massachusetts. He wanted to keep some ties to his home state. The new vacation home was spacious enough for his large family, which now included an eighth child, Jean Ann, born in 1928. Each summer, the children took swimming, golf, and tennis lessons and competed in sailing races. The home's huge lawns were perfect for the family's frequent games of touch football.

In June 1929, the family moved to its permanent residence, a new estate in Bronxville, New York. Although the stock market crashed in October of that year, ruining the financial security of many Americans, Joseph Kennedy had sensed a change coming in the nation's economy. He had wisely sold off most of his stocks by that spring. Unlike many other Americans, he lost none of his fortune.

Jack changed schools again in 1929. This time he

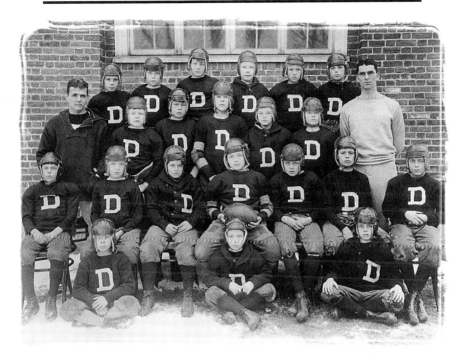

The Dexter School football team. John is seated in the bottom row (on the ground), on the far right; Joe, Jr., is in the second row, third from the left.

enrolled at Canterbury Preparatory School, a Catholic boarding school in New Milford, Connecticut. Jack began with high marks in English, math, and history, but struggled in Latin. However, he had to leave school when his appendix needed to be removed. He made up his work with the help of tutors and passed his final exams.

In the fall of 1931, Jack joined his brother Joe, Jr., at the Choate School, a boarding school in Wallingford, Connecticut. Sons of wealthy and powerful families attended Choate. Jack's cheerful personality made an instant impression on the staff and students. At fourteen, he was painfully thin, but that did not stop him from

SOURCE DOCUMENT

a Plea for a raise
By Jack Kennedy

Dedicated to my
Mr. J. P. Kennedy

Chapter I

My recent allowance
is 40¢. This I used for areoplanes
and other playthings of childhood
but now I am a scout
and I put away my childish
things. Before I would spend
20¢ of my ¢ allowance
and in five minutes I
would have empty pockets
and nothing to gain and
20¢ to lose. When I a
a scout I have to buy

Although he was wealthy, Joseph Kennedy knew the value of a dollar. To encourage his children to budget their money, he kept their allowances low. Here, young Jack makes a plea for a raise.

canteens, haversacks, blankets, searchlights, poncho, things that will last for years and I can always use it while I can use a cholcolate marshmellow sunday with vanilla ice cream and so I put in my plea for a raise of thirty cents for me to buy scout things and pay my own way more around.

Finis

John Fitzgerald Francis
Kennedy

competing fiercely in sports. He was too small to excel in varsity football, but he did make the junior squad. He also competed in basketball, baseball, crew (rowing), and golf.

Unfortunately, Jack's intense dislike for routine caused problems. His sloppiness wound up irritating his roommate. The headmaster, George St. John, wrote Joseph Kennedy to complain that rules bothered his son. St. John added that Jack "had a great deal of natural ability, but is careless in applying it."[8]

The ninth and last Kennedy baby was born to Rose and Joe on Washington's Birthday in 1932. He was named Edward Moore Kennedy, after one of Joe, Sr.'s business associates. The family called him "Teddy."

At this time, many people in America were feeling the results of the Great Depression, the worst economic downturn in our nation's history. Many people were out of work. Many more people were finding difficulty making ends meet. The Kennedys, however, were so well off that Joe, Sr., purchased a third home, a sprawling ocean-front estate in Palm Beach, Florida.

Joseph Kennedy now changed his focus from business to politics. He told his friend, singer Morton Downey, "In the next generation, the people who run the government will be the biggest people in America."[9] In 1932, he decided to support Franklin D. Roosevelt's presidential campaign. In return for Kennedy's financial and political support, Roosevelt appointed him to be the chairman of the new Securities and Exchange Commission (SEC). The SEC is the government agency that regulates the stock market.

In the fall of 1934, Joe, Jr., began his freshman year at Harvard University in Cambridge, Massachusetts. Jack, finally out from under his older brother's shadow at the

Choate School, began to shine. He showed a real flair for writing. Unfortunately, illness again caused him setbacks. In February of his junior year, he became alarmingly thin and broke out in a rash of hives. Doctors thought these might be symptoms of a serious blood disease or hepatitis, a liver disease. Eventually, he was sent home, where he spent the rest of the term. When he returned to Choate in the fall, Jack was not allowed to participate in vigorous athletics.

In February 1935, Jack was nearly expelled from Choate. He had formed the Muckers Club with his close friend Lem Billings and eleven other students. *Muckers* was a word the headmaster often used to describe students who did not try hard enough or who misbehaved.

The Kennedy family enjoys the summer of 1931 at their home in Hyannis Port. Left to right: Robert, John, Eunice, Jean, Joseph, Rose, Patricia, Kathleen, Joe, Jr., and Rosemary. (Edward "Teddy" was not born yet).

23

Headmaster St. John viewed the club as a personal challenge to his authority. He threatened to expel the club members if they did not disband. St. John summoned Jack's father to Choate for a conference. At this meeting, Joe, Sr., cautioned his son about the seriousness of his behavior and the need for change. However, afterward, in private, his father congratulated Jack on the creativity of the club, and, for the first time, praised Jack's leadership abilities.[10] Jack agreed to dissolve the club, so he was not expelled. He also learned a very important lesson: His father would support him, no matter what.

Jack successfully completed that final school year. He passed all his exams and graduated in 1935 in the middle of his class. To win the award of "most likely to succeed," Jack persuaded his fellow Muckers to campaign on his behalf.[11] He also traded votes with other boys who wished to be named "the best dancer," "the handsomest," or the best in some other category.[12]

Next Jack was expected to study for a year at the University of London, just as Joe, Jr., had done. However, no sooner had Jack started at the London School of Economics in the fall of 1935 than he fell ill again. This time, he was struck with a serious attack of jaundice, a symptom of hepatitis, or liver disease. The most recognizable sign of jaundice is yellow skin, caused by a build-up of yellow fluids in the liver. Jack's poor health caused him to go home in October.

Once home, Jack felt better. He enrolled at Princeton University in New Jersey. His friend Lem Billings was a student there. The decision to attend Princeton was made independently of his father, who had indicated a preference for his son's enrolling at Harvard. However, Jack's liver problems flared up again. He withdrew from school and rested at the Jay 6 Ranch near Benson, Arizona.

In the fall of 1936, Jack agreed with his father that he should go to Harvard after all. He was feeling better, but he looked frail. Standing six feet tall, he weighed only 149 pounds. At Harvard, Joe, Jr., was already a leader on campus. As in the old days, Jack tried to compete for attention. However, Joe was elected to student council, whereas Jack lost his election for the same office. The following year, Jack ruptured a spinal disk in his back while playing football. This injury added to the back problems that had already troubled him all his life.

Up to this point, Jack had not concentrated on his studies at Harvard. His father wrote to the dean, "Jack has a very brilliant mind for the things in which he is interested, but is careless and lacks application in those in which he is not interested."[13] However, for the first time, Joe Kennedy noticed that Jack was beginning to show signs of ambition and more interest in his studies. Jack, too, recognized that during his sophomore, or second, year in college, he was finally beginning to apply himself.[14] His developing ambition soon showed itself in an interest in world affairs.

3

THE COMING OF WAR

In December 1937, President Franklin D. Roosevelt appointed Joseph Kennedy ambassador to the Court of St. James's in London. The appointment made him the official United States ambassador to Great Britain. Kennedy was the first American of Irish descent to be named to this position.

Jack took a leave of absence during his junior year at Harvard to join his family in London. In February 1939, he traveled in Europe, doing research for his planned senior thesis. The topic he chose was Great Britain's lack of preparation for war. His early selection of this thesis topic showed a decisiveness new to his character.[1] However, when he finally wrote and typed the paper, he enlisted the help of people in his father's office. This delegation of responsibility was typical of his method of solving problems and represented Jack's lack of organization and his easy boredom with routine tasks.[2]

Jack (left) and K. LeMoyne "Lem" Billings visit the Hague in the summer of 1937. The trip was for fun, but it developed Kennedy's interest in international affairs. The dog is Kennedy's dachshund Offie.

Meanwhile, unrest was growing in Europe. World War II broke out on September 1, 1939, when Adolf Hitler's German armies attacked Poland. England and France, the Allies, declared war on Germany, but did not offer any assistance to Poland. Joseph Kennedy feared conditions were becoming increasingly unsafe for his family in London, so he sent them all home to the United States.

Jack graduated from Harvard in June 1940. That fall, his thesis was published as a book entitled *Why England Slept*. Joseph Kennedy used his contacts in the publishing world to help locate a publisher for the book. Arthur Krock of *The New York Times*, a close friend of Jack's father, helped Jack edit his manuscript before it was published. Joseph Kennedy's personal speechwriter checked the project's grammar and spelling.[3] The timely publication of *Why England Slept* at the start of World War II helped the book become a best-seller. Jack remained proud of this literary effort his entire life.

Unsure of his career plans, Jack decided to enroll at the Stanford University School of Business Administration in Palo Alto, California. Jack took two courses, one in political science and one in government. Quickly popular with young women at the school, he enjoyed off-campus life and had many dates.

Whereas Jack was still uncertain about his career objectives, Joe, Jr., was already well on his way toward a career in politics. Although only twenty-four years old, Joe was chosen as part of the Massachusetts delegation to the Democratic National Convention, where delegates from throughout the nation would choose the next Democratic party nominee for president.

Tensions increased worldwide in September 1940

John F. Kennedy's senior thesis at Harvard University was published as a book, Why England Slept, *just before America's entrance into World War II. Because the book discussed Great Britain's lack of preparedness for war, its publication was timely.*

when Japan signed the Tripartite Pact. With this pact, Japan formed an alliance with Germany and Italy.

On October 16, 1940, Jack registered for the military draft. Seventeen million other American males from the ages of twenty-one to thirty-five were also required to register. President Franklin D. Roosevelt and his advisers were now acknowledging the possibility that the United States might become involved in World War II. Many military troops would be needed.

Joseph Kennedy felt that there were no good economic reasons to fight a war.[4] In his position as ambassador, he officially expressed serious doubt that Great Britain could ever defeat Germany. His comments infuriated the British. Some of his friends suspected he had political ambitions of his own to run for president against Roosevelt in 1940.[5] In any case, the negative publicity his comments received forced him to resign as ambassador in February 1941. Any political plans Joseph Kennedy might have been entertaining for himself were now ruined. To make up for his own dashed hopes, Joe, Sr., became determined that Joe, Jr., should become a leader in politics.

Jack's sister Rosemary, the oldest Kennedy daughter, had been born with mental retardation. Unfortunately, by 1941, Rosemary's behavior had become aggressive and unpredictable. Joseph Kennedy arranged for her to undergo a lobotomy, a type of brain surgery, which doctors hoped would calm Rosemary. Today this type of procedure is considered inhumane, but at the time, a lobotomy was an accepted "cure" for her condition. Unfortunately, the surgery left Rosemary with the mental capabilities of a four year old. She was sent to live in a special home in Wisconsin. At that time, mental retardation was considered shameful. The family decided to keep Rosemary's condition a secret.[6]

That spring, Jack relaxed by touring South America. When he returned to the United States, President Roosevelt had declared a "state of national emergency."[7] The probability of American troops fighting in World War II was growing.

The two oldest Kennedy sons wanted to enlist in the military. Although Joseph Kennedy did not want the United States to become involved in World War II, he put the support of his sons' wishes ahead of his personal views. Joe, Jr., had enlisted in the Naval Aviation Cadet Program.[8] His enlistment presented a challenge to Jack, since the brothers had always engaged in friendly competition. When Jack failed the physical for the Army Officers Candidate School, he enlisted his father's help in finding a doctor who would give him a passing mark on the United States Navy physical. On September 25, 1941, Jack was commissioned as an ensign in the United States Navy and obtained a position in naval intelligence. Jack's job was to prepare daily and weekly bulletins from the information received from foreign sources.

Jack lived in Washington, D.C., close to his sister Kathleen, who had become known as "Kick" because of her bubbly personality. Kick worked as a reporter on the *Times-Herald* newspaper.

One of Kick's fellow reporters was a Danish woman named Inga Arvad. When he met her, Jack was immediately attracted to her, although she was not yet divorced from her second husband. Arvad had also associated with Adolf Hitler and other high-ranking German officials. The Federal Bureau of Investigation (FBI) suspected she might be a spy. Jack was in danger of being discharged from the Navy because of his affair with Arvad. Instead, he was finally reassigned to Charleston, South Carolina, and the relationship with Arvad ended.

In December 1941, America officially became involved in World War II when the Japanese attacked the American forces in Pearl Harbor, Hawaii. Like many other young men his age, Jack desperately wanted to be on active duty. In July 1942, he began training to command a patrol torpedo, or PT, boat.

PT boats were speedy, lightweight wooden craft used to surprise the enemy at night. PT boats traveled deep into enemy territory and returned from their missions by sunrise.[9] By cutting back the power of their three engines, they could quietly move in on their targets and fire their torpedoes without warning.

By September 1942, Jack had been promoted to the rank of lieutenant junior grade. He did so well during his PT-boat training session that he was made an instructor. However, Jack wanted to go to sea, and early in 1943 he got his wish. He was shipped to the Solomon Islands in the South Pacific. He was stationed on the island of Tulagi and served through November 1943.

Kennedy's roommate, Johnny Iles, sized up Kennedy as a good officer who kept his crew organized and his boat shipshape.[10] Iles was certain, even then, that Jack Kennedy would amount to something someday. He commented, "It was written all over the sky that he was going to be something big. He just had that charisma."[11]

Kennedy commanded PT-109, with a crew of twelve. This was Kennedy's first experience as a leader and exposed him to a variety of people who came from backgrounds less privileged than his own.

Every other night, Kennedy and his PT-109 crew went out on patrol, looking for Japanese warships. The Japanese had a base called Vila on nearby Kolombangara Island. They shipped troops and supplies to this base at night, sailing through the New Georgia Sound.

On the evening of August 1, 1943, PT-109 cruised in the Blackett Strait, on the west side of Kolombangara. Kennedy's boat was part of a group of fourteen PT boats searching for Japanese destroyers. At about two o'clock in the morning on August 2, a crewman in the front of PT-109 suddenly spotted a dark shape about two hundred yards away. It was the Japanese destroyer *Amagiri*, bearing

Lieutenant John F. Kennedy, skipper of the PT-109.

straight for them. Kennedy tried to turn the wheel of his boat to avoid hitting the destroyer, but the huge *Amagiri* rammed right into PT-109. Two of its crew members died instantly. Kennedy was tossed against the side of the boat. The force of the collision exploded the PT boat's gas tanks, sending gasoline flames skipping over the water and shattering the boat. Later, Kennedy recalled that he felt certain he was going to die.[12]

Part of PT-109 stayed afloat. Kennedy and his ten surviving crew members, wearing life jackets, clung to the remnants of their boat, hoping to be rescued. However, by daybreak, what remained of the hull of PT-109 began sinking. Kennedy ordered his crew to swim to an island about three miles to the southeast. Crewman Pat McMahon was unable to swim on his own because he had been badly burned in the explosion. By clenching the strap of McMahon's life jacket between his teeth, Kennedy was able to tow him. It took nearly five hours for the crew to reach what turned out to be Plum Pudding Island. Then, when the exhausted men reached the island, they found it had no food or water, only coconut trees.

Kennedy kept up his crew's spirits. He later helped them swim to another island to improve their chances of rescue. He also explored the island and found a small amount of food that had been hidden by the Japanese. Kennedy's actions led to the crew's rescue. Using his jackknife, he scratched a message on a coconut shell to explain the crew's position. Kennedy gave the coconut to two natives, who took it to Lieutenant Arthur Evans, an Australian naval coast watcher, or lookout. As a coast watcher, Evans's job was to perch in a secret outpost high atop a volcano on the island of Kolombangara and radio

Kennedy, standing on the far right, poses with some of his crew members early in July 1943, before the sinking of PT-109.

the Allies when he spotted enemy warships. When he received the inscribed coconut shell, Evans sent natives to bring Kennedy back to Evans's base. When Kennedy and his surviving crew arrived there safely, they radioed the United States PT base to arrange for their rescue.

After the rescue, Kennedy was hospitalized for a week in the naval hospital on the island of Tulagi. He suffered from a backache, an ear infection, and numerous sores caused by cutting himself on coral reefs. Kennedy's commanding officer wanted to send him back to the United States for a new assignment. Such an arrangement was routine when a boat had sunk. But Kennedy wanted to take command of a new boat immediately. He was determined to get even with the Japanese for destroying PT-109.[13] His commanding officer believed that Kennedy also felt guilty that he had lost his ship and two of his men.[14]

By October 1, Kennedy had taken command of PT-59. It was soon converted to Gunboat #1 by removing its torpedo tubes and attaching large machine guns to the bow, or front of the boat. This conversion gave Gunboat #1 greater firepower with which to attack the Japanese barges carrying supplies to their bases.

However, Lieutenant Kennedy's back and stomach began to cause him increasing distress. He weighed barely 145 pounds and was also suffering from malaria, a serious tropical disease. In addition, a Navy medical officer diagnosed Kennedy with the beginnings of an ulcer, or open sore in the stomach's lining. In December 1943, he was sent back to the United States. X rays showed that Kennedy had injured a disk in his back. Since major back surgery was recommended, the Navy granted him time off to rest.

In June 1944, Kennedy received the Navy and Marine Corps medal for his ". . . extremely heroic conduct . . ." that had "contributed to the saving of several lives. . . ."[15] Although he was hailed as a hero, some fellow PT skippers felt that Kennedy had shown faulty judgment in losing PT-109.[16] Perhaps he could have maneuvered the boat better and avoided the accident. Perhaps the crew was not as alert as it could have been: Two men were asleep and two were lying down at the time of the collision.[17]

Whatever the case, Kennedy stuck with his men and showed a heroic spirit in rescuing them. Kennedy always remained modest about his efforts. Years later, when asked by a high school student how he became a hero in the South Pacific, he replied, "It was easy—they sank my boat."[18]

Award-winning author John Hersey wrote about the PT-109 incident in the June 17, 1944, issue of *The New Yorker* magazine. As a result, Kennedy's fame spread.

Joseph Kennedy made the most of his son's PT-109 adventure. In mid-June 1944, he convinced *Reader's Digest* to publish a condensed version of Hersey's original article. He made sure his son's leadership would be stressed. Later these articles would become an important part of the publicity campaign for John F. Kennedy's political career.

Events during World War II deeply affected Jack's family. In the ongoing competition with his older brother, Jack succeeded in going into battle first, holding a higher rank, and winning a medal. Rose Kennedy said later, "I expect this was the first time Jack had won such an 'advantage' by such a clear margin. And I daresay it cheered Jack and must have rankled Joe, Jr."[19]

After Jack's exploit, Joe, Jr., felt enormous pressure to prove his bravery. He volunteered for a dangerous bombing mission to France, which was occupied by German troops. Joe, Jr., piloted a bomber packed with over twenty thousand pounds of high explosives. The target was the German rocket-launching sites in France that fired rockets at England. Before his plane reached enemy territory in France, Joe was supposed to bail out over the English Channel, leaving the plane on automatic control and aimed at the target. Before he could bail out, however, the plane accidentally exploded. Twenty-nine-year-old Joseph Kennedy, Jr., died on August 12, 1944.

Then, less than a month later, Kick's husband, an English nobleman, William Cavendish, Marquess of Huntington, died in battle.

During these tragedies, Jack was recuperating in the

Chelsea Naval Hospital in Boston, where he had undergone surgery to try to correct his spinal disk problem. After operating, doctors told Jack they did not think his back condition could ever be cured.[20] These continuing back problems led to Jack's discharge from the Navy with the rank of full lieutenant.

The months following his brother's death were a difficult time. Jack felt that now his father would always consider his brother superior to him, that there was no way left to compete. Jack was now the oldest son. He wondered what role his father expected him to fill.[21]

Jack took positive action to work out some of his and his family's grief. He asked twenty close friends and family members to write down their remembrances of Joe, Jr. Jack wrote a foreword and assembled the essays into a book entitled *As We Remember Joe*. Privately published in 1945, the book was given to relatives and friends. Joseph Kennedy was extremely touched by the project.

Ever since the incident at Choate involving the Muckers Club, Joseph Kennedy had recognized Jack's leadership qualities.[22] With Joe, Jr., dead and his own political chances ruined, Joe, Sr., focused on Jack as the family's best hope for a future politician.[23] Joseph Kennedy had long dreamed that a Kennedy could become the first Irish-Catholic president. Now Jack Kennedy would be groomed to fill the role.

4

GOING TO
CONGRESS

While the Kennedy family dealt with their grief, World War II was coming to an end. The Allies—the United States, England, France, and Russia—were on their way to defeating the Axis powers—Germany, Italy, and Japan.

In February 1945, President Franklin D. Roosevelt met with British prime minister Winston Churchill and Soviet leader Joseph Stalin. "The Big Three" agreed to accept a plan for a new postwar international peacekeeping organization, known today as the United Nations (U.N.). Unfortunately, President Roosevelt did not live to see the end of the war and the establishment of the U.N. He died on April 12, 1945.

A conference to plan the United Nations was scheduled for April 25, 1945, in San Francisco, California. Covering the conference as a journalist would be a good way for Jack Kennedy to get publicity for future political races, so over the course of three months, he did just that, writing sixteen articles for a chain of newspapers owned by the Hearst family.

In June, the Hearst organization sent Kennedy to London to cover the British elections. The next month, he went to Potsdam, Germany, where he covered the postwar conference attended by the new American president, Harry Truman; British prime minister Winston Churchill; and Soviet premier Joseph Stalin. The Potsdam Conference centered on issues affecting the rebuilding of Europe. One item was setting Germany's boundaries. After the conference, Germany remained divided into eastern and western zones. Eventually, the western zones united into West Germany, a democracy friendly to the United States. The eastern zone became East Germany, with a Communist government friendly to the Soviets. During these negotiations, Stalin refused to give up any of the territory Russian troops had occupied in Poland during the war. Stalin's behavior hinted at worsening relations between the United States and the Soviet Union.

In early August, Kennedy fell ill again. Several Navy doctors diagnosed the illness as a flare-up of malaria. However, the condition may actually have been Addison's disease, an affliction of the endocrine system which gradually destroys the adrenal glands, causing them to produce insufficient amounts of certain hormones. One result is a reduced immunity to illness, which often leads to death because of the body's lowered ability to fight infections. Symptoms of Addison's include weight loss, a yellowish skin tint, and poor appetite, all of which Kennedy displayed.

During the last weeks of the summer of 1945, Jack Kennedy and his father began seriously to discuss entering politics. Joe Kennedy was determined that his son should run for public office. Years later, Jack told reporter Bob Considine, "My father wanted his eldest son in politics. 'Wanted' isn't the right word. He demanded it."[1] At Christmastime, Jack Kennedy agreed to run for public office.

Joe Kennedy felt certain that his son should run in Massachusetts, where the Fitzgeralds and the Kennedys had a tradition of political leadership. In April 1946, Jack Kennedy announced his decision to run for the congressional seat from the Eleventh District. This was the same seat his grandfather, John Francis "Honey Fitz" Fitzgerald, had held. Joe, Sr., hoped his own relationship with Fitzgerald, his father-in-law, would win votes for his son.

Kennedy lacked confidence in his ability to speak unrehearsed, or to ad lib, preferring instead to have the aid of a written text of a speech. Even so, he appealed to his listeners, especially when he smiled.[2] His obvious sincerity and natural charisma attracted many voters. Kennedy built a large volunteer organization. "There was something about his personality that made you want to drop whatever you were doing and go to work for him," said his aide, Dave Powers.[3] Kennedy worked to make his campaign workers feel important.[4]

Of course, Jack enjoyed the support of the entire Kennedy family. His father controlled funds and worked behind the scenes of the campaign. For example, he used his contacts in the publishing industry to encourage *Look* magazine to feature Jack in an article. It appeared in the final weeks of the congressional campaign. Joe also arranged for one hundred thousand reprints of John

Hersey's PT-109 article to be mailed to voters. Since Jack Kennedy was the only military veteran in the race, it made sense to stress his war record.

Jack's sisters Eunice, Pat, and Jean planned teas. Twenty-five to seventy-five people attended each one. So did Rose Kennedy, who attracted many female voters, eager to rub elbows with someone of Rose's social stature and curious to observe up-close her fabled designer clothing and upper-class manners. Rose had been her father's political hostess, so she was a confident speaker. She spoke as if she knew her listeners personally, sharing anecdotes about the challenge of raising a large family. Jack Kennedy also sparkled at such events. He seemed to form a natural bond with his listeners.

The steady accelerated pace of the campaign, however, was brutal. Jack met workers at factories and called on voters door-to-door. Each evening, he tried to attend at least six parties in private homes. Typically he got only four or five hours of sleep each night. Yet Kennedy soon found that he enjoyed campaigning more than he had expected.

This initial campaign, the Eleventh District congressional race, set the pattern for each of Kennedy's future campaigns. The activity level was high and electric. A great deal of money was spent, and his father orchestrated its spending. Still, in the end, it was not just Kennedy's family money, but his natural charm, interest in people, and dedication that won him many votes. In the Democratic primary in June, Kennedy defeated the other nine candidates by winning 42 percent of the vote. In November, he won by a landslide over his Republican opponent.

Now twenty-nine years old, Representative John F. Kennedy moved to Washington, D.C. He rented a house in

Georgetown, an upscale section of the city. He lived with his sister Eunice, who worked as an executive secretary of the Juvenile Delinquency Committee of the Justice Department. She also served as his official hostess. Kennedy gave many parties and soon earned a reputation as an extremely eligible young bachelor.[5]

In Congress, Kennedy was appointed to the House Committee on Education and Labor and to the subcommittee of the House Veterans' Affairs Committee. Better working conditions and housing for veterans were two of their goals. Kennedy also wanted a higher minimum wage. These issues were important to his constituents, the people he was elected to represent, back home in Massachusetts' Eleventh District.

Jack Kennedy never really reached his stride in the United States Congress. He remained more absorbed by national and international affairs than by matters concerning his own district. He lacked interest in the daily operations of the House of Representatives. His new personal secretary, Mary Davis, worked for him for six years. She noted that he "never did involve himself in the workings of the office. He wasn't a methodical person."[6] His numerous absences and sloppy style of dress annoyed some of his colleagues. Sometimes he even wore sneakers and old khaki pants on the floor of the House.[7]

During the congressional summer recess of 1947, Kennedy planned to visit Western Europe and Russia. There he would study education and labor conditions with fellow members of the House Committee on Education and Labor. On the way, he stopped in Ireland to visit the county where the Kennedy ancestors had been born. He spent time with his sister Kick, who was living at Lismore

The newly elected congressman takes a break at the Hyannis Port beachfront house in 1946.

Castle, an estate in County Waterford belonging to the family of her deceased husband. Kick had invited several houseguests whose company she thought her brother would enjoy. Among them were British statesman Anthony Eden and Kick's friend Pamela Churchill, the ex-wife of Winston Churchill's son Randolph.

After a month's stay in Ireland, Kick and Jack Kennedy accompanied their friend Pamela to London, where she lived. Kick journeyed on to Paris, where she and her mother enjoyed a shopping spree at the latest fashionable salons. Kennedy's plan was to travel from England to meet his congressional colleagues on the European continent. However, while still in London, he collapsed with symptoms of severe nausea and low blood pressure. His physician there, Sir Daniel Davis, definitively diagnosed Addison's disease, thereby confirming what had been suspected two years before. Davis told Pamela Churchill, "That young American friend of yours, he hasn't got a year to live."[8] Kennedy was given injections of desoxycorticosterone acetate (DOCA), a synthetic hormone. DOCA increases the activity of the adrenal glands to produce more hormones. Then Kennedy's doctor implanted DOCA pellets in his thighs. The pellets released the needed hormones into his bloodstream each day. From then on, Kennedy had the pellets replaced every two to three months. He was also given cortisone pills, which increased his stamina and his appetite. This medication also made his face fill out, helping to improve his frail appearance. The doses of DOCA and cortisone allowed Kennedy to maintain a normal activity level.

For the rest of Kennedy's life, the family kept supplies of DOCA and cortisone in safe-deposit boxes around the United States. That way, Kennedy would never be caught without the medicine he needed. However, the family tried to keep his condition a secret. Kennedy never wanted the public to think that he might have a physical handicap that could prevent him from serving in high office.[9]

Tragedy struck the Kennedys again in 1948. On May 13, Kick was killed in a plane crash. Her death affected Kennedy deeply, because she was his favorite sister. For months afterward, Kennedy thought and talked often about death. His battle with Addison's disease coupled with the recent deaths of Joe, Jr., and Kick caused him to reexamine his goals. Childhood friend Lem Billings explained that it was during this period that Kennedy finally focused on what he wanted to do with his life, and "he realized that it really might be politics after all."[10]

He finished his first term in Congress and campaigned again in 1948 with renewed vigor. Voters in his district reelected Kennedy in both 1948 and 1952. In all, he served three terms as one of Massachusetts' delegates to the House of Representatives.

In January 1951, he went on a five-week trip to Europe to study issues related to the defense of Western Europe, and it broadened his background in foreign affairs. He visited European nations that, along with the United States, belonged to the North Atlantic Treaty Organization (NATO), a regional defense alliance formed in 1949. After World War II, many western nations considered the policies of the Soviet Union (USSR) to be threatening to peace in Western Europe. The Soviets had installed Communist governments similar to their own in the Eastern European nations of East Germany, Poland, Czechoslovakia, Hungary, Romania, Bulgaria, and Albania. (Another nation, Yugoslavia, had also become Communist, but was not under Soviet control.)

As a result of differing ideologies, a struggle developed between the United States, together with its allies, and the Communist nations aligned with the Soviet Union. This struggle involved intense economic and diplomatic conflict—without actual warfare. Thus, it was called the Cold War. However, both the United States and the USSR were developing atomic weapons and were continuing to compete with each other in what became known as the arms race, or who could collect the largest amount of military weapons. Jack Kennedy felt that strengthening the defense of Western Europe would be the best way to prevent the spread of communism and to curb the influence of the Soviet Union.[11]

In May 1951, on his return from Europe, Jack Kennedy was invited to a dinner party at the Washington, D.C., home of his friends newspaperman Charles Bartlett and his wife, Martha. There Kennedy was introduced to a strikingly attractive, cultured young woman named Jacqueline Bouvier. Bartlett had

> a feeling that these two were very special. Jackie had a sort of quiet glamour about her and Jack was a young, gangling fellow with unusual charm, and I just thought it [their relationship] might be good. I felt they would compensate each other in ways that were exciting enough to hold the other's interest.[12]

Jackie was born in Southampton, on Long Island, New York, on July 28, 1929. Her father, John Vernou Bouvier III, was a wealthy Wall Street stockbroker, and her mother, Janet Lee Bouvier, came from a high-society background. Jackie's childhood was divided between New York City and East Hampton on Long Island, where her family had an estate called Lasata. Jackie brought home many first-place blue ribbons from horse jumping competitions in the Hamptons. With her active imagination, she loved making up stories, reading, writing poetry, and sketching.

Her parents divorced in 1940, and two years later, her mother married Hugh D. Auchincloss, who owned homes in McLean, Virginia, and Newport, Rhode Island. Jackie attended Miss Porter's School for Girls in Connecticut, a prestigious boarding school for wealthy young women. At Vassar College and then at the Sorbonne in Paris, where she spent her junior year, Jackie excelled in history, literature, and the study of the French language. She also spoke

Igor Cassini, a well known society columnist for the Hearst newspaper chain, named Jacqueline Bouvier Debutante of the Year in 1947.

fluent Italian and Spanish. Jackie had transferred to George Washington University in Washington, D.C., and was a senior there studying French literature when she met Jack Kennedy.

Although Jackie was twelve years younger than he, Kennedy recalled that, unlike most other women he had dated, Jackie seemed to have more purpose in life than just trying to look beautiful.[13] At the Bartlett dinner party, her intellect was quickly apparent. After the meal, the dinner guests played word games. Kennedy excelled at such games, but in Jackie, he had met his match. She performed even better than he did. Duly impressed, Kennedy asked her if she wanted to go out for a drink after the dinner party. Jackie declined, since another young man was waiting to drive her home. Still, Kennedy called the Bartletts the next day to find out more about her.

However, both Jack and Jackie were apparently too busy to pursue their relationship at that time. Jack was occupied with his legislative duties and visiting constituents. Jackie completed her degree in French literature in 1951 and spent the summer in Europe with her sister, Lee Bouvier.

Upon her return, Jackie got her first job. She was hired as a newspaper reporter to write a column called "Inquiring Camera Girl" for the Washington, D.C., *Times-Herald*. In this job, she approached total strangers, asked them questions about current issues and events, and took their pictures.

That winter, she and Jack Kennedy began to date regularly, often going to small dinner parties given at the homes of the Bartletts or Bobby and Ethel Kennedy, Jack's brother and sister-in-law, who also lived in Georgetown. Favorite activities after these dinners included playing Monopoly, Chinese checkers, and bridge.

By this time, Jack Kennedy was preparing to take on a new challenge, running for the United States Senate.

5

SENATOR KENNEDY

Jack Kennedy was ready for a change. He had been a congressman for six years. He still found the day-to-day procedures in the House of Representatives to be tedious and frustrating. So many congressmen and too many rules made the passage of legislation slow. In addition, the Kennedy family tradition of setting high goals seemed to require that Jack move on. Seeking a seat in the United States Senate was the next logical step in an eventual search for the presidency. It offered a better opportunity to gain the necessary background and strength in broad national and international issues, which had always seemed more interesting to Kennedy than local and domestic policies.

Kennedy was now in his midthirties. His ability to ignite the imagination of voters was becoming increasingly apparent. Although the efforts of his extended family to

50

affect the outcome of his three previous election campaigns remained important, Jack Kennedy was emerging as a powerful leader in his own right. The natural charm and wit he had possessed since childhood proved to be helpful tools for the political arena. In addition, he was starting to build a reputation as an expert in foreign affairs. He was well-traveled and well-read. As a result, Kennedy began to question his father's narrower, more provincial outlook on national and international affairs.

In April 1952, Kennedy announced his candidacy for the United States Senate from Massachusetts. His Republican opponent was the current senator, Henry Cabot Lodge, Jr. Lodge came from another prestigious Massachusetts family: His grandfather had also been a politician. In 1944, Lodge had resigned his Senate seat to serve in the United States Army in Europe. He earned the Bronze Star and several other decorations for bravery during World War II. Battling Lodge would be tough. Still, Joseph Kennedy told his son, "When you've beaten him, you've beaten the best. Why try for something less?"[1]

Lodge started the campaign at a disadvantage. He was busy leading a group of Republicans who wanted General Dwight D. Eisenhower, commander of the Allied forces in World War II, to resign from the United States Army and become the 1952 Republican nominee for president. While working to develop support for Eisenhower, Lodge spent much time away from his Senate duties, which Kennedy was quick to point out to voters. His efforts on behalf of Eisenhower also kept Lodge from beginning his own senatorial campaign until two months before the election.

Furthermore, the Lodge campaign could not match the personal commitment of the Kennedy campaign. In

1916, Lodge's grandfather had beaten Jack Kennedy's grandfather, John Francis Fitzgerald, for the same Senate seat. Kennedy was determined to avenge his grandfather's loss. In addition, the Lodge family was part of the same Massachusetts social class that had denied Joe Kennedy admittance into its top financial and social circles. Thus, Jack Kennedy's campaign also came to represent his father's ongoing battle against the leaders of the social establishment.[2]

Joseph Kennedy got behind the senatorial campaign with his typical energy and financial support. However, Joe, Sr., kept a low profile and made few campaign appearances, because his publicized views on world affairs during World War II left him unpopular. People still remembered Joe's opposition to the war and his lack of confidence in Great Britain's ability to beat Nazi Germany.

Joe was also known for his outspoken criticism of some of his son's campaign workers. Jack decided he would need a family member to manage not only the campaign but also his father. For this job, he chose his brother Robert, who was known as Bobby. Because he was eight years younger, Bobby had not been particularly close to Jack when they were children. However, as the brothers became adults, they became increasingly close, especially as Bobby's interest in politics and government grew. Bobby had graduated from Harvard University and earned a law degree at the University of Virginia. He was working in the Internal Affairs Division of the Justice Department, but he quit this job in 1952 to manage Jack's campaign. Bobby threw himself into the campaign, proving himself to be an energetic, effective campaign manager. However, he alienated some campaign workers by expecting them to work as hard as he did. Nevertheless, Jack appreciated his brother's loyal support and total dedication.

The Kennedys decided to continue the tradition of tea parties begun in the 1946 campaign. Hand-addressed, engraved invitations were sent to thousands of women.[3] Each tea was held in a fancy hotel, so that it would look like an exclusive party, not a political reception. At each tea, Jack and at least one of the Kennedy women mingled intimately with the guests. The teas were a decisive factor in exposing voters directly to the Kennedy charisma.

As always, sixty-year-old Rose Kennedy attracted attention with her enthusiasm and impeccable elegance. During "Coffee with the Kennedys," a call-in television program shown twice during the campaign, she appeared with her daughters and answered viewers' telephone calls about Jack's childhood. She also gave numerous speeches to church and civic groups, speaking engagingly about Jack's and Joe, Jr.'s war records and the challenges of raising a large family.

Jack Kennedy campaigned in every city and town in Massachusetts. The long hours driving by car and standing to give speeches were hard on his back. Sometimes he had to use crutches for support. Kennedy lived on fast food—cheeseburgers and malts. Voters found Kennedy's intelligence and lively demeanor attractive. He always remembered people's names. Ultimately, his hard work and winning personality won him 51.5 percent of the vote. The new senator was only thirty-five years old when he was sworn into office on January 3, 1953.

In 1978, years after Kennedy's senatorial victory, his opponent, Henry Cabot Lodge, Jr., praised him: "[Kennedy] had a tremendous and well-deserved popularity and he

Representative John F. Kennedy campaigns on crutches for a seat in the United States Senate. His mother, Rose Kennedy (right), was already a seasoned campaigner.

was an extraordinarily likable man. In fact, I liked him. So often in a campaign you look for a man's faults and then campaign on them. Well, in this case, you didn't do that."[4]

In January 1953, Dwight D. Eisenhower was inaugurated as president of the United States. Jack Kennedy, along with all the other United States senators, was invited to the inaugural ball. His date was Jacqueline Bouvier. Since April 1952, they had been dating as often as his busy campaign schedule would allow. While out on the campaign trail, Kennedy telephoned Jackie to set up dates for the times he would be back in Washington, D.C. Jackie commented that their courtship was "conducted mainly at long distance with a great clanking of coins in dozens of phone booths."[5]

With his father's insistence, Jack Kennedy had decided that the time was right in his political career to find a wife and start a family. Jack knew Jackie was more intelligent and socially prominent than the other young women he had dated.[6] Jack cared about Jackie, although he did not display his affection publicly, nor was he one for sending her flowers or candy.[7] Still, the couple had many things in common. Both enjoyed history and sailing. Each had an acid wit and liked to gossip about their friends. Both were excellent listeners, skilled at drawing individuals into conversation. However, Jackie disliked both politics and athletics. Nevertheless, Jack admired her ability to speak foreign languages, and she impressed him with her knowledge of music and the arts. He made up his mind that she would be his wife.

Early in January, Kennedy made another momentous decision. He hired Theodore "Ted" Sorensen as his legislative aide. Although only twenty-four years old, Sorensen was a gifted writer who, from that point on, crafted many flowing speeches and well-written articles for his boss.

In the meantime, Kennedy kept up his courtship of Jacqueline Bouvier. When she was in London covering the June 2, 1953, coronation of Queen Elizabeth II, Jack proposed by telegram. He told Jackie that he had known all along that she was the one he wanted to marry.[8] However, he asked if they could postpone the announcement of their engagement until after an article about him, "Jack Kennedy—The Senate's Gay Young Bachelor," would appear in *The Saturday Evening Post* in mid-June.

The wedding took place on September 12, 1953, in Newport, Rhode Island. The wedding reception was held at Hammersmith Farm, an estate owned by Jackie's stepfather, Hugh Auchincloss. It was one of the most exclusive and talked-about social events of the year.

Jackie made an instant hit with her father-in-law. Joe Kennedy admired Jackie's poise and clever wit. He also correctly calculated her overwhelming potential to help his son's political future. Soon Jackie came to depend on her father-in-law's support and encouragement. They talked often about a variety of subjects and made each other laugh.[9] Their bond was so close that Jackie commented, "Next to my husband and my own father, I love him more than anybody—more than anybody in the world."[10] On the other hand, Jackie often irritated her mother-in-law, Rose. Like her new husband, Jackie failed to follow traditional social structure. She loved sleeping late in the morning and was often tardy to functions. Jack's sisters made fun of Jackie's breathy voice, large feet, and lack of athletic ability.

Quickly, Jackie helped shape up her husband's manners

and improve his taste in clothes. Jack soon began to wear neatly pressed shirts. Finally, his suit coat matched his pants. Jackie also broadened Jack's exposure to and interest in the arts.

The couple enjoyed each other's company. A friend described Jackie's influence: "He really brightened when she appeared. You could see it in his eyes; he'd follow her around the room watching to see what she'd do next."[11]

Nevertheless, the couple's first year of marriage proved challenging. Jackie often irritated her husband with her carefree attitude toward spending money.[12] For example, she changed their kitchen wallpaper three times in a three-month period. However, Jack worked long hours, and on weekends he traveled, making speeches to voters throughout Massachusetts. He often left Jackie home alone. It was widely rumored that Jack continued to be involved in New York City's social scene.[13] Some of his letters and telegrams now on file in the Kennedy Library show he maintained an interest in other women.[14] His father's openly adulterous lifestyle had never set Kennedy a good moral example.

Throughout these years, Kennedy continued to suffer from terrible back pain. By the middle of 1954, he was having trouble walking, even with the aid of crutches. He considered having surgery to fuse several vertebrae in his back to alleviate the problem. However, doctors advised Kennedy against having surgery because his Addison's disease would lower his resistance to infection. Still, Kennedy remained determined to undergo the operation. He told Jackie, "I'd rather be dead than spend the rest of my life on crutches."[15] On October 11, 1954, he was admitted to the New York Hospital for Special Surgery in Manhattan. His doctors took X rays and conducted medical tests needed to plan Kennedy's surgery.

Finally, the surgery took place on October 21. At first, the operation appeared to be successful. Then, three days later, Kennedy contracted an infection that did not respond to treatment with antibiotics. Close to death, he was given extreme unction, a rite of the Catholic Church. However, his body slowly fought off the infection on its own, and he was taken off the critical list.

While Kennedy was recovering, a controversy raged in the Senate. It regarded Wisconsin senator Joseph McCarthy, an old family friend. Like Kennedy, McCarthy was strongly anticommunist. McCarthy had gradually become more and more outspoken in his views. He accused people of being Communists, even though many were not. He thrived on the publicity that these accusations earned him. He warned against "Communist sympathizers," or people who tolerated Communists' views. McCarthy ruined the careers and lives of many innocent individuals with his accusations. The Senate finally decided to take a vote on whether or not to censure, or publicly condemn, McCarthy for his unfair and disruptive actions. If Jack Kennedy voted to reprimand McCarthy, he would, in effect, be defying his father. The back surgery proved to be a blessing. Because he was in the hospital recovering on December 12, 1954, when the vote was taken, Kennedy was able to avoid facing the dilemma. Although he could have arranged to have his views made known, he did not.

On December 21, 1954, eight weeks after the surgery, Kennedy was released from the hospital. He was transported by stretcher and private ambulance to LaGuardia

Airport in New York City. From there, he and Jackie flew to his parents' Palm Beach estate. There an entire wing of the house was turned into what resembled a suite of hospital rooms. During her husband's recuperation, Jackie spent hours reading to Jack and playing checkers and Monopoly™ with him. Her positive attitude throughout this ordeal earned her the respect of the entire Kennedy family.[16]

By February, Kennedy needed another operation because of a second infection. After that surgery, he slowly began to heal. News reports blamed his wartime injuries for causing his illness and operations. This was not strictly true; however, these reports made for excellent publicity and public sympathy.

During his second recovery, he kept busy with a writing project. Kennedy wrote about several senators, including John Quincy Adams and Sam Houston. These men had all taken strong stands on controversial issues at the risk of their careers. Perhaps Kennedy had been motivated to cover this subject by dwelling on his own cowardice in facing the McCarthy vote. The book that resulted from this project, entitled *Profiles in Courage*, quickly made the best-seller list in 1956. Its literary success boosted Kennedy's already thriving national reputation. The scholarly work seemed to set the young senator apart from other less idealistic politicians.

Later, in 1957, *Profiles in Courage* won the Pulitzer Prize for biography. However, a controversy developed over the award. Kennedy's assistant, Ted Sorensen, and several well-known historians had assisted in the research and preparation of the book, yet Kennedy claimed sole authorship of the work. According to historian Herbert Parmet, at best Kennedy should have called himself the editor and overseer of the project, instead of taking credit for being its sole writer.[17]

On May 23, 1955, Jack Kennedy returned to the Senate. His fellow senators gave him a warm welcome. Vice-President Richard Nixon arranged for a basket of fruit and candy to be placed on Kennedy's office desk with a note on it reading "Welcome Home."[18] At a press conference, Kennedy wanted to convince reporters that he was fully recovered, so he told them he had thrown away his crutches. In reality, within a few days, he had to consult a doctor for pain.

In the late summer of 1955, in connection with his work on the Senate Foreign Relations Committee,

Kennedy autographs copies of his book Profiles in Courage, *which won the 1957 Pulitzer Prize.*

Kennedy went on a nine-week European tour. Jackie accompanied him and served as his interpreter when he met French premier Georges Bidault.

When they returned to the United States in October, the couple purchased two residences. One was a vacation home in Hyannis Port, Massachusetts. It was part of the Kennedy family compound, or group of several residences surrounded by a privacy wall. The second was Hickory Hill, a large manor on six acres in McLean, Virginia.

Although Kennedy now appeared to be an established married man, he was still having difficulty settling down. His prominence in the Senate and his boyish good looks caused many young women to be attracted to him. FBI records note relationships he had with other women between 1955 and 1959.[19] However, Jack and Jackie maintained a happy appearance in public, and newspaper stories portrayed them "as a modest, hardworking, and romantic" couple.[20]

Jackie was experiencing her own set of difficulties adjusting to married life. She still resented her husband's consuming interest in politics and the almost constant presence in their home of his political colleagues. Old friends like Lem Billings were often houseguests. She also felt frustrated that she was not yet able to have a baby.[21]

In August 1956, when Jack Kennedy arrived at the Democratic National Convention in Chicago, he was already a celebrity. Publicity for *Profiles in Courage* had built up his public image as an intellectual and a best-selling writer. He had been chosen to narrate a film used to open the convention. His role in the film and the national television coverage of the proceedings of the convention now made him known to millions more Americans, and suddenly

Jack Kennedy found himself under consideration as a candidate for the vice-presidential nomination. He came close to achieving the nomination, but lost out to Senator Estes Kefauver of Tennessee. Although disappointed, Kennedy gave his official support to presidential nominee Adlai Stevenson of Illinois. His humble manner in getting behind the Stevenson-Kefauver ticket earned him the respect of his party along with valuable national publicity.

The race for the vice-presidential spot on the ticket also taught Kennedy a valuable lesson in politics. Just after the convention, he confessed to Dr. Janet Travell, the physician who had been treating his back problems, that he was disappointed about losing the nomination, but that he had learned "that it should be as easy to get the nomination for President as it was for Vice President. Until then, I thought I would have to work first toward the vice presidency."[22]

After the convention, Kennedy took a break and went yachting on the Mediterranean Sea. He usually took such a trip each August after Congress adjourned. Jackie, who was eight months pregnant, wanted her husband to stay home and help her get ready for the baby. However, Jack felt he needed time off after all his hard work at the Democratic convention.[23] While Jack was overseas, Jackie gave birth to a stillborn baby girl. Kennedy did not return home until three days after the baby's death. He had not been reachable by telephone on the yacht. His bad timing strained the Kennedys' already tense marriage and earned him negative publicity.

Both parents were deeply saddened by the baby's death. Jack, along with the other Kennedy men, loved children and dearly wanted to have a family of his own. Joe

Kennedy makes an appearance at the 1956 Democratic convention, where he was an unsuccessful candidate for the vice-presidential nomination.

Kennedy told a friend, "Jackie losing the baby has affected him [Jack] much more than his illness did during that bad year. . . ."[24] Jackie felt doubly frustrated when she compared herself with the other Kennedy women, who seemed to have no difficulty having children. She could no longer bear to live at Hickory Hill, where she had decorated a nursery especially for the new baby. Also, it reminded her of all the lonely nights when her husband had been out campaigning or spending time with other women.[25] So Jack and Jackie sold the estate to Bobby and Ethel Kennedy and moved into a rented home in Georgetown.

As rumors of an impending divorce spread, Joe

Kennedy stepped in to try to repair the relationship. Peter Lawford, a movie actor who was married to Jack's sister Patricia, said that Jackie and Joe had a meeting during which Joe reassured her that Jack loved her even if his conduct did not always seem to show it.[26] Soon *Time* magazine reported that Joe Kennedy, hoping to avoid a scandal, had offered Jackie $1 million not to divorce Jack.[27] Family friend Igor Cassini confirmed the rumor that Joe Kennedy had offered a financial incentive to Jackie. Cassini stated that Joe Kennedy told him that a divorce would ruin his son's political career.[28] Other rumors circulated that Joe had asked Jackie to stay with Jack through his eventual presidential campaign.[29]

Whether or not Joe actually offered Jackie money, it seems clear that he did step in to try to smooth over his son and daughter-in-law's relationship. The couple soon made changes to reduce some of the strains on their marriage. The demands of a political career meant that telephone calls and meetings would often interrupt meals and other family events. Jack agreed that he would no longer take telephone calls during dinner. Vacation times spent at Hyannis Port had never been totally relaxing, since the entire Kennedy clan lived at a frantic pace and ate all their meals together. Now Jack and Jackie agreed that when they were at Hyannis Port, they would eat dinner with the extended family only one night a week, a decision that met with Joe Kennedy's approval.

That November of 1956, Jack Kennedy decided the time was right to make his move for the next presidential election in 1960. He held a respected and highly visible position in the Democratic party. The publicity for *Profiles in Courage* had built his image as an intellectual. Voters were impressed with his war record. He made an excellent appearance on television, a medium of growing importance in politics. Funding a campaign would never be an obstacle, not with his family's wealth. At that time, planning a presidential campaign so far in advance was a bold step. However, by January 1957, a group of Washington news reporters had already rated Kennedy as the top contender for the 1960 Democratic party nomination for president.[30]

In March, Jackie learned that she was once again expecting a baby. In hopes that this pregnancy would be a safe one, Jackie planned to limit all travel and activities that would cause her stress. Instead, she focused on redecorating the Georgetown home the Kennedys had just purchased. Jackie loved decorating, and in the interest of family harmony, Jack now encouraged her by placing no limits on the amount of money she could spend. Jackie spent hours researching colors, patterns, and fabrics, selecting items that would appeal to both of them.

For some time, Kennedy had hoped to be appointed to the Senate Foreign Relations Committee, one of the most powerful bodies in the Senate. Committee members discussed issues relating to American involvement in foreign affairs. Jack Kennedy knew he had to build a national reputation if he wanted to be president, and the Foreign Relations Committee presented a perfect forum for this purpose. The committee would provide Kennedy with an opportunity to speak out on international issues and gain national publicity. In 1957, Democratic Senate majority leader Lyndon B. Johnson from Texas named Jack Kennedy to the committee.

More national publicity came from Kennedy's participation on the McClellen Committee, a special Senate committee formed to investigate illegal behavior by labor unions. Kennedy's brother Bobby was the lead counsel, or head lawyer. While Jack was a member of the committee, the brothers uncovered illegal connections between high-ranking labor leaders and members of organized crime. Jack Kennedy's name frequently appeared in the news tied to a valiant fight against crime in labor movements.

On November 27, 1957, Jack and Jackie became proud parents when Caroline Bouvier Kennedy was born. The baby's birth strengthened the Kennedy marriage. Lem Billings recalled, "Jack was more emotional about Caroline's birth than he was about anything else."[31]

A public opinion poll taken in mid-1958 showed that the public overwhelmingly considered Jack Kennedy the most admired man in the Senate.[32] In 1958, he won reelection to his Senate seat with over 73 percent of the vote. This was the greatest margin of victory any candidate had ever achieved in Massachusetts history. The stage was set for John F. Kennedy to pursue the nomination for president of the United States.

6

THE ROAD TO THE PRESIDENCY

On January 2, 1960, John F. Kennedy announced his candidacy for president of the United States. Kennedy felt that the key issues facing the country were ending the arms race with the Soviet Union, improving science and education, and increasing the nation's economic growth.

Kennedy enjoyed several advantages as a candidate. He had plenty of money to finance an election race. His winning personality and youthful enthusiasm aroused devotion in campaign workers. As a bonus, he had not been part of the losing Democratic presidential ticket in 1956.

However, many Democratic party leaders did not support his candidacy. Eleanor Roosevelt, the widow of President Franklin D. Roosevelt, questioned Kennedy's qualifications. She felt he had shown a lack of character by failing to make clear his position on the McCarthy controversy.[1] Others objected to Kennedy's youth and his relative inexperience, as well as to his Roman Catholic faith.

Kennedy's key opponent for the Democratic nomination was Minnesota senator Hubert Humphrey. To win the party's nomination, a candidate had to win the most votes in a series of primary elections held in several states. The winner of each state primary earned the votes of all that state's delegates to the national party convention.

Kennedy easily won the first primary election, which was held in New Hampshire. The next race was in Wisconsin, a state neighboring Minnesota. Humphrey was considered the favorite because of his strong following in the region. Although Kennedy won in Wisconsin, the victory was not decisive. He lost in Protestant districts but won in Catholic ones. Therefore, it was clear that the issue of Kennedy's religion remained a factor in the primaries. Humphrey decided he might still have a chance to win the nomination. He entered the next primary, to be held in West Virginia.

From the start of the West Virginia race, Kennedy's religion caused uncertainty. The nation had never elected a Catholic president. Voters wondered whether or not Kennedy, if elected, would take direction from the pope, the head of the Catholic Church. Kennedy responded to these rumors of bigotry: "I am a Catholic, but the fact that I was born a Catholic, does that mean that I can't be the President of the U.S.? I'm able to serve in Congress and my brother [Joe, Jr.] was able to give his life, but we can't be President?"[2] Kennedy pointed out that his congressional record showed clearly that he did not follow orders from the pope.[3] On the contrary, he opposed federal aid to

Kennedy, vacationing in Half Moon Bay, Jamaica, poses with fellow American tourists, losing no opportunity to campaign before the 1960 Democratic convention.

religious schools. He was also against sending a United States ambassador to the Vatican in Rome, the headquarters of the Catholic Church.

It was difficult for Humphrey to compete with the powerful Kennedy resources. Humphrey traveled in a rented bus and flew on commercial airlines. Kennedy had his own private jet, the *Caroline*. Kennedy posters and bumper stickers vastly outnumbered those for Hubert Humphrey. In the end, Kennedy won forty-eight of West Virginia's fifty-five counties, and Humphrey withdrew from the presidential race.

By the end of May 1960, young Senator Kennedy had won seven Democratic primaries altogether. It looked as if he would be the frontrunner for the presidential nomination at the Democratic National Convention that July.

Then a new, more experienced candidate entered the race. Five days before the convention opened on July 11, Senator Lyndon B. Johnson, the Senate majority leader, announced his candidacy. In his brief campaign, Johnson tried to compare forty-two-year-old Kennedy's youth and inexperience with his own twenty-three years in Congress. Johnson also played up Kennedy's health problems. Kennedy countered, stressing the importance of youthful "vigor" as a desirable quality for an American president. (Kennedy's Boston accent caused him to pronounce the word as "vigah.") Johnson's supporters felt Kennedy's references to vigor were an unfair indirect attack on Johnson's own health problems (he had suffered a severe heart attack in 1955) and his ability to govern. Despite Johnson's strong record of party leadership, Kennedy won the party's nomination on the first ballot.

Throughout the primaries and the beginning days of the Democratic convention, Johnson had shown no interest in the vice-presidential nomination. Insiders who had worked closely with Johnson suspected he would never give up his powerful position as Senate majority leader to be vice-president.[4] However, although Johnson may have been jealous of what he considered to be Kennedy's unearned star status in the Democratic party, Johnson was first and foremost a practical politician. His own ambition was so great that it caused him to consider all alternatives. Surely he considered the undeniable fact that if the president died, he would be next in line for the presidency.[5] In any case, the vice-presidency was a sure way to gain national prominence, useful perhaps for a future presidential race.[6]

Joseph Kennedy sized up all these factors, too, and thus, having weighed all the pluses and minuses, suggested Johnson as a natural choice for vice-president. Johnson's solid experience as a statesman and his Texas roots would lend a nice balance to the ticket. He would attract southern voters, while Kennedy would draw those from New England. Then only a few more electoral votes would be needed to win the election. No Democrat had ever been elected president without receiving a majority of votes from the South.[7]

Jack Kennedy knew Johnson looked down on him as a political novice, but Kennedy wanted to work toward party unity. However, his brother Bobby opposed choosing Johnson as the vice-presidential candidate. Bobby, in fact, had already told many delegates that Johnson would not be on the ticket.[8] Bobby was angry that Johnson and his aides had questioned his brother's health. Nevertheless, despite Bobby's opposition, Jack Kennedy asked Lyndon Johnson to join the ticket. Joe Kennedy reassured his son, saying, "Don't worry, Jack. In two weeks everyone will be saying that this was the smartest thing you ever did."[9]

In only fourteen years, Jack Kennedy had risen from a first-term congressman to the Democratic party nominee for president of the United States. In his acceptance speech in front of the convention, Kennedy emphasized his vision of the future. He called it the "New Frontier."[10] For this New Frontier, Kennedy proposed economic reforms and a plan to "get the country moving again."[11] His legislative goals called for medical aid for the elderly, a higher minimum wage, and increased federal funding for education, housing, and transportation. Kennedy likened his New Frontier to Franklin D. Roosevelt's New Deal. Roosevelt had rescued the nation from the Great Depression with this New Deal in the 1930s.

In August 1960, the Republican party nominated Richard M. Nixon, the current United States vice-president under Dwight Eisenhower, as its presidential nominee to run against Kennedy. As Nixon's running mate, the Republicans chose Henry Cabot Lodge, Jr., the same man Kennedy had handily defeated in his 1952 Massachusetts Senate race.

As usual, all the Kennedy family members threw themselves into the campaign. Robert Kennedy served as his brother's campaign manager. Edward "Teddy" Kennedy campaigned in the west. Rose made public appearances in fourteen states, and Jack's sisters hosted numerous teas. Jackie Kennedy, pregnant with another baby due in December, did not travel with her husband. However, she wrote a newspaper column describing her experiences during the campaign. It appeared in many newspapers nationwide under the headline "Campaign Wife." Jackie also appeared on the *Today* show, and she taped campaign messages in several languages for radio and television. Joe Kennedy purposely kept a low profile to preserve the myth that he was not involved in the campaign. In truth, he supported it fiercely with funds and advice.

The two presidential candidates were not far apart on the issues. Both supported a strong military. They sensed that the relationship between the United States and the Soviet Union was a crucial matter. After World War II, the Soviets had increased their military might until the Communist USSR and the democratic United States now stood as the world's two superpowers. The Soviet Communists were determined to expand their influence

SOURCE DOCUMENT

PUBLICITY DIVISION
DEMOCRATIC NATIONAL COMMITTEE
1001 CONNECTICUT AVENUE, N.W.
WASHINGTON 6, D.C.

FOR RELEASE ON RECEIPT

September 16, 1960
B-2357

Following is the first of a series of weekly columns by Mrs. John F.
Kennedy. These columns will be mailed to any newspaper on request. A
two-column mat of a heading carrying the title of the column, Campaign
Wife, on a photograph of the Kennedys and their daughter will be supplied
on request. Write Public Affairs Division, Democratic National Committee,
1001 Connecticut Avenue, N.W., Washington 6, D.C., to receive this column
on a regular weekly basis.

CAMPAIGN WIFE

By Mrs. John F. Kennedy

For the first time since Jack and I have been married, I have not
been able to be with him while he is campaigning. You can imagine how
frustrating it is to be in Hyannis Port reading all that he's doing and
not participating in any way. This week I decided one way to keep from
feeling left out was to talk through this column to the friendly people
all over the country I would have met while campaigning. Just in the few
weeks of being with Jack in Wisconsin and West Virginia I met so many
people whom I would still like to be in touch with.

The worst part was not being in Los Angeles for the nomination.
To me it seemed it would surely be better to be there than sitting anxiously
by the television in Hyannis Port, but my obstetrician firmly disagreed.
Since then I have resigned myself and have kept up with my husband by
reading several newspapers every day and by writing to Jack's many
friends throughout the country.

*Jacqueline Kennedy, who was pregnant, stayed at home
while her husband hit the campaign trail. However, she
wrote this newspaper column entitled "Campaign Wife"
during the 1960 presidential campaign.*

worldwide. Americans were frightened by the Soviets' technological superiority. The Soviets were leading in the field of space exploration and had also developed nuclear missiles. Many Americans feared the "missile gap," or the difference between the size of America's arsenal and the Soviet advantage in the number of missiles owned. It was not surprising that much of the nation feared the outbreak of nuclear war with the Soviets. Both Kennedy and Nixon stressed the need for the United States to be a world leader in opposing communism and to win the Cold War, or the ideological conflict between the two superpowers.

A series of four television debates between the two presidential candidates began in late September. Nixon claimed that his experience as vice-president under President Eisenhower had given him outstanding qualifications to serve as president. He pointed out that his dealings with Soviet premier Nikita Khrushchev and other international leaders made him an experienced statesman. He emphasized the importance of private business and limited government control. Kennedy stressed that his vision of the New Frontier offered limitless possibilities and renewed optimism to the nation. He felt that America's economic weakness could be improved through government action. Kennedy also expressed his desire for freedom worldwide.

Those who listened to the debates on the radio felt Nixon performed better than Kennedy. But television viewers considered Kennedy the winner. They found him to be poised, polished, and handsome. Nixon, on the other hand, sweated in his stage makeup and appeared to need a shave. He had recently been hospitalized for two weeks with a knee infection and looked pale.

Kennedy and Richard Nixon (left) engaged in a series of debates during the 1960 presidential campaign. Kennedy's winning personality and confidence came across clearly on television.

Kennedy used the medium of television as a new political tool. As such, the debates ended up serving as free publicity for his campaign. Seventy million voters were exposed to his polished image for the first time and came away captivated by his smooth performance and easy manner. Voters flocked to hear him at future campaign appearances. The debates had countered the Republicans' contention that Kennedy was an inexperienced political novice.

Civil rights became an important campaign issue since race relations were changing. In 1957, Martin Luther King, Jr., and others had formed the Southern Christian

Leadership Conference (SCLC). King became a leader in questioning and eventually removing racial barriers. He helped African Americans to be assured of their right to vote and to obtain educational opportunities equal to those of whites.

Neither Kennedy nor Nixon expressed a strong position on civil rights for African Americans. They feared antagonizing white voters, especially in the South. However, a small action by Kennedy won him the support of many African Americans. On October 19, 1960, Dr. King and fifty-one other protesters were arrested in Atlanta, Georgia, after a civil rights demonstration. At first neither Nixon nor Kennedy took a strong stand on King's arrest. Then Kennedy telephoned King's wife, Coretta Scott King, to tell her that he had been thinking about her and Dr. King. Kennedy still did not take a strong position on the actual arrest, but his friendly sympathy was better than Nixon's silence. King was soon released from jail and thanked Kennedy for his support. King's response boosted Kennedy's popularity among African-American voters.[12]

On November 8, Election Day, Jack and Jacqueline Kennedy went to the polls in Boston and voted. Then they traveled to Hyannis Port to await the election results. At first, the CBS and ABC television network computers projected Nixon as the winner. Soon, however, the computers reversed their position, projecting that Kennedy would win with 51 percent of the vote. But as results trickled in, neither candidate was taking a clear lead. Kennedy went to bed in the early hours of the morning, still unsure of the results. Finally, at about two o'clock in the afternoon on November 9, Kennedy was declared the winner. It was the narrowest margin of victory of any presidential election in the century. John Fitzgerald Kennedy was now the first Roman Catholic ever elected president, and at age forty-three, the youngest.

The Kennedy family gathered at the National Guard Armory in Hyannis Port, where Jack made his victory speech. The newly elected president, with his pregnant wife by his side, promised to prepare for a new administration. The new baby seemed to symbolize both the first couple's youthfulness and the dawn of a new political era.

Kennedy, who as president-elect quickly became known as JFK, spent Thanksgiving Day with Jackie and Caroline in their Georgetown residence in Washington, D.C. That evening, Kennedy boarded the *Caroline* to fly to Palm Beach to do some work. Two hours later, Jackie was rushed to the hospital. Kennedy was notified in midflight that his wife was in labor. He told his special assistant Kenneth "Kenny" O'Donnell, "I'm never there when she needs me."[13] Kennedy landed in Florida and boarded a faster plane to return to Washington. Over his radio, the pilot received word of the birth of John F. Kennedy, Jr. John-John, as the baby was soon affectionately called, spent the first five days of his life in an incubator, a device that offers special care to premature babies. His proud father visited the infant in the hospital three times a day for the next two weeks.

Kennedy was deeply disappointed by his narrow margin of victory. He had won only 49.7 percent of the vote, compared to Nixon's 49.6 percent. More than ever, he became determined to prove his effectiveness as president.[14] Kennedy started by building a well-qualified staff. He chose his brother-in-law, Eunice's husband, R. Sargent Shriver, to find "the brightest and the best" people to fill his Cabinet and approximately twelve hundred other appointed positions.[15] Kennedy selected people of such outstanding qualifications that he seemed to be staffing a university, not a government of politicians.[16] In fact, he chose as advisers many teachers and scholars, such as McGeorge Bundy and Arthur M. Schlesinger, Jr., both from Harvard University. His most influential aide was Ted Sorensen, who had worked for Kennedy since he was a senator. Many of Kennedy's appointees were Republicans, like Secretary of Defense Robert McNamara, former president of the Ford Motor Company.

The Cabinet appointments fit the Kennedy image of youth, vigor, and brilliance. The average age of the Cabinet was forty-seven, ten years younger than President Eisenhower's Cabinet. The youngest member was Attorney General Robert Kennedy, the president's thirty-four-year-old brother. The attorney general heads the Department of Justice and is the chief law enforcement officer of the United States. He represents the nation in court cases and functions as its main legal adviser. Controversy arose in the press over Bobby's appointment because he was so young and had never actually practiced law. At first, both Kennedy brothers had hesitated to appoint Bobby. However, their father had insisted that Jack needed at least one Cabinet member whose loyalty he could count on, no matter what.[17]

7

LIFE IN THE WHITE HOUSE

A n air of intense expectation filled Washington, D.C., on Inauguration Day, January 20, 1961. The anticipation resembled the nation's mood in 1933 when President Franklin D. Roosevelt began his New Deal. The night before John F. Kennedy's inauguration, eight inches of snow had blanketed the nation's capital. But snow drifts and the frigid twenty-degree temperature could not ruin the festivities. Poet Robert Frost stood to read a poem at the swearing-in ceremony. The sun glared off the snow so strongly that Frost could not see the words he had written. He ended up reciting his poem "The Gift Outright" from memory.

Kennedy, the first president born in the twentieth century, was determined to show off his famous youthful vigor. He did not wear an overcoat or hat while delivering his inaugural address. Kennedy called on Americans to bear the responsibilities of liberty. He delivered his now-famous line "My fellow Americans: ask not what your country can do for you—ask what you can do for your country."[1] Many voters, especially young people, were ready to answer this inspiring call to action.

A parade followed the inauguration ceremony. President Kennedy's favorite part was a float modeled after PT-109. It carried his old crew, who saluted him as they motored past. The new president waved back enthusiastically. Several inaugural balls took place that evening. Jackie, soon to become a fashion icon, looked lovely in a designer gown of white chiffon.

No sooner had Kennedy assumed the presidency than he involved himself in the struggle for civil rights.[2] His first

President and Mrs. Kennedy, flanked by Vice-President Lyndon and Lady Bird Johnson, accept congratulations from well-wishers at one of the inaugural balls, held at the Mayflower Hotel.

action occurred right after the inaugural parade. He noted that no African Americans had marched in the honor guard representing the United States Coast Guard Academy. The next day, the Academy was called to make sure that African Americans were admitted there and would be included in all future honor guard delegations.

According to Harris Wofford, President Kennedy's special assistant for civil rights, Kennedy had shown only limited interest in civil rights issues before becoming president.[3] He did not know many African Americans when he was growing up. However, he had supported most major civil rights legislation in his congressional career because he appreciated the basic fairness of ensuring equal rights to all races and religions. During his presidential campaign, he had reached out to Coretta Scott King for the same reason. However, he was not without selfish motives: He realized that he needed the votes of African Americans to win the election.

Kennedy loved being president. He usually got up in the morning at about seven-thirty. A fast reader, he whizzed through several newspapers. After a hot bath, he dressed and ate breakfast. At about eight-thirty or nine, Kennedy walked to his White House office. He had carefully chosen the mementoes on display. Models of some of America's greatest sailing ships, such as the *Constitution*, were part of the decor. His desk, presented to President Rutherford B. Hayes by the British, was made of timbers from the H.M.S. *Resolute*, shipwrecked in 1852. Jackie had discovered the desk stored in the White House basement. On top of the desk, Kennedy displayed his PT-109 coconut shell, as well as books such as the Bible and a world almanac. He often joked about his job: "The pay is good and I can walk to work."[4] He was modest in not adding that he donated his salary to charity.

Kennedy took care of a great deal of business by telephone, because he could get information fast. At that time, telephones were not in common use in politics. For example, President Charles de Gaulle of France refused to have a single telephone installed during his term of office.

Midday the president enjoyed a swim in the White House pool. He followed the swim with exercises to help strengthen his back. Next came lunch, which was often a hamburger served on a tray. After an afternoon nap, Kennedy spent an hour or so alone with his wife while their children napped.

At the end of each afternoon, Kennedy left the door to his office open. This action signaled to staff members that they could drop in to visit, share concerns, or ask questions.

On a typical day, he might see as many as seventy visitors. A television appearance or several telephone conferences would be common occurrences. It was not unusual for unexpected visitors such as foreign students to come by, and Kennedy usually found a few spare minutes to visit with them. Most days, he would have less than an hour to himself in the Oval Office, during which time he dictated memos or letters.

Many evenings he took home work, file folders full of materials to read and papers to sign. On other nights, formal, or state, dinners took place. These social events became more relaxed under the Kennedys than they had been before. The first couple did away with the traditional formal receiving line, during which the host and hostess had to shake hands with each guest.[5]

The Kennedys especially enjoyed giving small dinner parties for close friends, followed by a film in the White House movie theater. The theater had a special chair that allowed the president to lie back to view the screen. This position rested his back. However, if the film did not grab Kennedy's interest, he would usually leave the room after twenty or thirty minutes.

The president supported the first lady in her major project, a badly needed restoration of the White House. She sorted through more than twenty-six thousand pieces of furniture and furnishings that were stored in the White House basement and attic. Gradually, Jackie restored historic authenticity to the mansion. She convinced private donors to contribute many antiques. To raise additional funds for the furniture purchases and renovations to the mansion, she oversaw the publication of a guidebook that visitors to the White House were able to purchase. Sales of the book, *The White House: An Historic Guide*, continue today. Jackie also conducted a televised tour of the White House, which CBS broadcast on February 14, 1962. More than 50 million Americans viewed the program, for which Jackie received an Emmy award. As a result of her efforts, the number of visitors to the White House increased dramatically.

Weekends the Kennedy family often flew to Hyannis Port, where they stayed in their beach house near Joseph and Rose's family compound. The president loved to sail and play golf there. Sometimes they flew to Palm Beach. Forty miles west of Washington, D.C., was Glen Ora, a six-hundred-acre estate that the Kennedys had rented as a weekend getaway. There the president could relax and read, and the first lady could put on her

The Kennedy family poses on the porch of their vacation home in Hyannis Port in August 1962.

favorite old clothes and enjoy riding her horses across Glen Ora's expansive acres.

The family loved animals. Although the president was allergic to dogs, the Kennedys always had several. A favorite was the president's Airedale, Charlie. Other Kennedy pets included rabbits, guinea pigs, and two hamsters that often escaped from their cages. Caroline loved to ride her pony, Macaroni, on the White House lawn.

With their two young children, the Kennedys turned

Caroline regularly rode her pony, Macaroni, on the lawns of the White House grounds.

the White House into a lively and enchanting home. Caroline and John-John were the first young children to live there since Theodore Roosevelt's in the early 1900s. Kennedy sometimes took Caroline and John-John with him to the Oval Office. They loved to hide under their father's desk and to snatch candy from his secretary's desk. The president laughed when Caroline once walked into a press conference wearing her mother's high heels. Kennedy lamented that his bad back prevented him from

The president plays with John, Jr., and his toy horse on the White House porch in 1963.

lifting up his son and tossing him in the air, a game that little John-John loved. But father and son often took baths together, playing with John-John's toy ducks in the water. Caroline and John-John went to nursery school and kindergarten in the White House. Their mother had arranged special school classrooms on the top floor. Outdoors the children had a trampoline, which Jackie also enjoyed using.

Their father's storytelling fascinated the children. In these tales, Caroline won horse races, and John-John sank a Japanese destroyer in his PT boat. Kennedy created a character called the White Whale, who liked to eat dirty sweatsocks. White Whale supposedly followed the

Kennedy enjoys Halloween 1963 in the Oval Office with Caroline and John, Jr.

presidential yacht on an ocean cruise. One day, Kennedy asked Franklin D. Roosevelt, Jr., a guest on the presidential yacht, to throw his socks overboard to the whale. Years later, Kennedy's friend Lem Billings said that the president's friends soon learned "that when Jack began telling Caroline about the White Whale it was time to move to another part of the yacht."[6]

Jackie tried to shield the children from publicity. She wanted Caroline and John-John to lead as normal a lifestyle as possible. However, the president annoyed his wife by encouraging the children to talk to reporters and by allowing their pictures to be taken by press photographers. He had quickly learned that the publication of such heartwarming photographs increased his popularity.[7]

The president was always comfortable with members of the press. He cultivated warm relationships with these men and women so that they would report favorably on his actions. He was the first president to deliver live press conferences on both radio and television. Kennedy felt certain that the publicity gained from such broadcasts would be well worth the risks of making any errors.[8] He was right: In these conferences, he impressed Americans with his good looks and his solid grasp of issues and facts. Kennedy held ten such press conferences in his first three months in office.

He held a total of sixty-four televised press conferences during his administration. Historian Herbert Parmet noted, "He sold himself even more than his views."[9] In effect, Kennedy became the first president to use television as a tool of public relations. Kennedy once commented, "We couldn't survive without TV."[10]

Many journalists were aware of the rumors circulating about Kennedy's continuing romances with other women.

However, in those days, reporters did not publicize a politician's private relations. The press considered what a politician did in private to be his own business. To the outside world, Kennedy continued to look like a devoted family man.

The Kennedys brought youth and culture to the White House. Compared with the stuffy events held during the Eisenhower administration, the Kennedys' parties seemed exciting and glamorous. Jackie was equally adept at planning a poetry reading; a party featuring the twist, a popular dance of the time; or a formal state dinner followed by a ballet performance by Margot Fonteyn and Rudolf Nureyev, the most famous classical dancers of their day. In July 1961, the Kennedys gave the first state dinner ever held outside the White House. It was in honor of President Mohammed Ayub Khan of Pakistan. The presidential yacht *Honey Fitz* and three Navy ships transported 132 guests from Washington to Mount Vernon, home of President George Washington, where guests dined by candlelight on White House china.

The Kennedys' interest in western artist George Catlin made his paintings famous. The first couple also sponsored a series of young people's concerts on the south lawn of the White House. Cellist Pablo Casals performed in November 1961. The Kennedys invited forty-nine Nobel prizewinners for dinner in April 1962. Kennedy called the group "the most extraordinary collection of talent, of human knowledge, that has ever been gathered together at the White House, with the possible exception of when Thomas Jefferson dined alone."[11] Other famed musicians who visited the White House were composers Leonard Bernstein, Aaron Copland, and Igor Stravinsky, and violinist Isaac Stern.

At a White House reception for Nobel prizewinners on April 29, 1962, Kennedy visits with author Pearl S. Buck. Jackie chats with poet Robert Frost, who wrote a poem especially for JFK's inauguration.

The White House quickly became known as "Camelot," a reference to the exciting court of King Arthur and his knights of the Round Table. With their aura of good taste, their sponsorship of the arts, and the prominence of their two beautiful children, the Kennedys seemed as close to royalty as any first family had ever been. The Kennedy "court" was bustling with artistic and intellectual creativity. More important, the "royal family" appeared to be leading their nation to a renaissance of good deeds.

8

BUILDING A NEW FRONTIER

K ennedy remembered his campaign promise to deliver a New Frontier of "responsibility" and "action."[1] On his very first day in office, the president signed Executive Order Number 10914. It doubled the amounts of food provided to 4 million needy Americans. By the end of January, his first month in office, Kennedy had taken action in nearly every area of concern to the American public. He sent 277 requests to Congress in his first one hundred days.[2]

However, Congress did not wholeheartedly support many of his proposals. Although the Democrats held a majority of seats in both houses, southern Democrats joined with conservative Republicans to block many programs related to social issues. For example, they defeated a Medicare bill to guarantee medical care for the aged and a bill to create a Department of Urban Affairs. In order to get a measure through Congress, the president often needed to convince a majority of legislators of its worth. Kennedy was not consistently willing to put in the time and effort needed to develop such support. He had demonstrated a similar lack of discipline in school and as a congressman.

Nevertheless, Kennedy did accomplish a few notable programs early in 1961. He created the Food for Peace program, which provided food shipments to needy nations such as India, Egypt, and Algeria. An average of nearly $1.5 billion worth of food was shipped each year during the Kennedy administration. He also created the President's Commission on Equal Employment Opportunity. It guaranteed equal opportunity for government jobs to all citizens, regardless of their race or religion. Another executive order established the Council on Youth Fitness.

On March 1, 1961, Kennedy issued an executive order that created the Peace Corps, an organized and trained body of American workers sent overseas to help developing nations deal with local economic and social problems. R. Sargent Shriver, Kennedy's brother-in-law, was named director of the organization on March 4. Many Peace Corps workers lived in primitive conditions among the people they served. They helped build schools and medical facilities and taught improved methods of farming. The idea of the corps held immediate appeal, especially to young people. By the end of 1961, almost one thousand volunteers were serving. During Kennedy's years in office, Peace Corps workers served in forty-seven different countries. At the time he signed up for Peace Corps service, one young man explained, "I'd never done anything political, patriotic, or unselfish because nobody ever asked me to. Kennedy asked."[3]

Kennedy's decisions about foreign affairs at this time were heavily influenced by his anticommunist views and the growing tensions of the Cold War. On March 13, 1961, he held a White House reception for Latin American diplomats, where he announced the establishment of the Alliance for Progress. The Alliance aimed to improve education and promote economic development in all Latin American nations except Cuba, which had become a Communist country when Fidel Castro took control of its government in 1959. By encouraging democracy in the rest of Latin America, the Alliance hoped to discourage growing Communist movements.

The Alliance for Progress reinforced Kennedy's strong moral stand against the spread of communism. Cuban Communists were particularly threatening to Americans, because their island was only ninety miles off the coast of Florida. In March 1960, Kennedy's predecessor, Dwight D. Eisenhower, had approved Central Intelligence Agency (CIA) plans to invade Cuba. During the remainder of the Eisenhower administration, the CIA continued to plan the invasion. In two meetings before Kennedy took office, Eisenhower discussed the invasion plans with the president-elect.

Eisenhower's purpose in invading was to cause dissatisfied Cubans to revolt against Castro and his Communist regime. In Guatemala, the CIA actually trained a small army of Cuban exiles to lead the invasion. It was hoped that Cubans still living on the island would join the exiled Cuban invaders in overthrowing Castro. Then they would take control of the government and oust the Communists in power. As the situation turned out, these beliefs of the Eisenhower administration were very naive.

When Kennedy took office, he was unsure whether to support the invasion plan. CIA chief of operations Richard Bissell and CIA director Allen Dulles assured Kennedy that the plan would succeed.[4] Bissell and Dulles wanted to use American ships, airplanes, and military personnel in the actual fighting. Kennedy refused. Still, Bissell and Dulles assumed that once the invasion was under way, Kennedy would change his mind.[5] Although the president still had some misgivings about the project, he remained convinced that "Communist domination in this hemisphere can never be negotiated."[6] He went along with the CIA's optimistic predictions for success and finally authorized the invasion. The invasion was one way he could put his anticommunist beliefs into practice. However, Kennedy insisted that there be no United States military involvement, and he retained the right to cancel the invasion up to twenty-four hours before it was scheduled to begin.

Unfortunately, the invasion was doomed from the start. The site chosen for the invasion was the Bay of Pigs on Cuba's southern shore. The area was surrounded by treacherous marshlands. Should something go wrong, the invaders would never be able to escape to safety in Cuba's mountains. CIA leaders planning the invasion withheld this information from Kennedy. Also, the Bay of Pigs was one of Castro's favorite fishing spots, so the people in the area were intensely loyal to him. They would probably have no reason to join the invading Cuban exiles and overthrow their leader.

On April 15, 1961, several old World War II bombers owned by the CIA bombed the Cuban air fields. They destroyed only five of the approximately fifty Cuban planes that were tied to the ground. However, the air attack served as a warning to Castro that the invasion would soon begin, and he quickly had more than two hundred thousand troops ready. That same day, at 1:45 P.M., President Kennedy gave his final approval for the landing at the Bay of Pigs.

Two days later, a CIA-led force of about fifteen hundred Cuban exiles approached the Bay of Pigs in various small landing craft. Many boats overturned or ran aground on coral reefs. The invading forces had no protection from the air, because President Kennedy had cancelled the second planned air attack, hoping to avoid any appearance that the United States was involved in the invasion. More than one thousand invaders were captured and imprisoned in Cuba; most of the rest were killed.

As a result of this international tactical blunder, President Kennedy's prestige suffered dramatically. The United States looked both helpless for having failed in their military mission and immoral for supporting the takeover of another nation. Historian Herbert Parmet wrote, "Suddenly the promising world of the New Frontier lost its credibility."[7] Kennedy felt betrayed by the CIA, which had obviously expected him to change his mind and send in military assistance. Several times after the invasion, he remarked to some of his advisers, "How could I have been so stupid?"[8] To his credit, Kennedy took total responsibility for the failed attack.[9] At a press conference on the Friday after the invasion, he said, "There's an old saying that victory has a hundred fathers and defeat is an orphan. . . . I am the responsible officer of this government."[10] As a result, public opinion turned around and began to support him. By the end of April, his popular approval ratings climbed to 83 percent.[11]

In the aftermath of the disaster, Kennedy came to rely ever more heavily on the advice of his brother Bobby, because he trusted him wholeheartedly. The president could count on his brother to tell him the truth, even when it was difficult to do so. On the other hand, the president would never again give so much power to the CIA. In fact, he replaced key CIA leaders whom he no longer trusted. However, he remained steadfastly opposed to communism—and to Castro's government.

In the 1960s, the United States was consumed with winning the space race with the Soviet Union. The Soviets had already launched Yuri Gagarin, the first man in outer space, on April 11, 1961. On May 5, 1961, the United States space program reached a positive milestone: Alan Shepard became the first American in space. Kennedy proposed that the United States land an American on the moon before the end of the decade. (This goal was achieved when mission Apollo astronaut Neil Armstrong stepped onto the moon on July 19, 1969.)

The Soviet Union had already expanded its influence into East Germany. In Southeast Asia, Communists supported local guerrilla movements attempting to take over the countries of Laos and Vietnam. Guerrilla soldiers did not fight in the typical way that armies had traditionally used for years. Instead, they relied on unconventional methods of warfare, including sneak attacks, using thick jungle growth for cover.

In Laos, between March and May 1961, Kennedy and his advisers worked to establish a cease-fire, or military order to stop firing. American troops and warships were sent near the area as a warning, but after the failure of the Bay of Pigs, Kennedy was fearful of sending troops into Laos.[12] A cease-fire between the Laotian government and the Communist guerrillas, known as the Pathet Lao, was signed in May, but it did not last long. The Pathet Lao, who were supported by the North Vietnamese, continued to send in troops. Kennedy promised Laos' neighbors, Vietnam and Thailand, that the United States would maintain support of their governments against Communist takeover. These promises eventually led to a secret—and later not-so-secret—war in Vietnam.

While the United States was busy fighting communism in Southeast Asia and Latin America, many significant changes were taking place at home, especially in the area of civil rights. Many schools, especially in the South, were still segregated. This meant there were separate classes or even separate schools for white students and African-American students. African Americans were also seated in separate sections from whites in restaurants and had to sit in the back of buses. Often they were not allowed to vote and were denied equal opportunities to obtain many jobs.

The time was ripe for the civil rights movement to blossom. Many African Americans had served their country during World War II and had received a broader view of the world. The African-American middle class also began to grow after the war. African Americans wanted equal access to better housing and jobs. In addition, many white Americans were becoming educated about and embarrassed by the centuries of injustices to African Americans. It would seem unfair for politicians to criticize Communist nations for violations of human rights when the United States did not treat all of its own citizens fairly.

Because of the increased awareness of racism in America, many college students had become interested in working for social change.

Leaders in the civil rights movement were making their voices heard. In December 1955, Rosa Parks, a forty-two-year-old seamstress, was arrested in Montgomery, Alabama. She refused to obey a law that required African Americans to give up their seats on buses to whites and move to the back. A year later, the Supreme Court ruled that racial segregation on public transportation was unconstitutional.

Dr. Martin Luther King, Jr., had become the most prominent spokesperson for African-American rights. His stirring speeches and participation in boycotts and sit-ins spurred action by both whites and African Americans. During a sit-in, protesters would refuse to move from non-segregated seats in a racially segregated establishment such as a restaurant. They would also refuse to cooperate when police tried to arrest them, sitting in place until the police had to move them physically from their positions.

The president and his brother, the attorney general, planned to improve civil rights by taking executive action.[13] They hoped to use the power of the presidency and the Department of Justice to support federal court rulings to end segregation and ensure the right to vote. They also worked toward equal opportunity in employment by requiring the federal government and corporations with government contracts to provide African Americans equal opportunities for jobs.

However, the president delayed acting on legislation to end discrimination in federally assisted housing. He needed the votes of southern white legislators to pass other measures, and he feared that by alienating these lawmakers, they would support nothing. Kennedy especially needed their backing in the areas of education, raising the minimum wage, and improving health care for the elderly. Kennedy felt he was not totally ignoring the plight of African Americans, since legislation in these other areas would benefit them as well as whites.[14] The president also hoped that by taking a minimum amount of action, he could satisfy some of the demands of both African Americans and white southern Democrats.

Kennedy had clearly underestimated the strong feelings African Americans had toward ending segregation. On

Martin Luther King, Jr. (left), and Attorney General Robert Kennedy (right) both worked to end racial segregation and ensure rights for African Americans.

May 4, 1961, two buses carrying both African Americans and whites left Washington, D.C., planning to arrive in New Orleans, Louisiana, by May 17. These "Freedom Riders," as they called themselves, were testing southern enforcement of the 1960 United States Supreme Court ruling against segregated bus terminals that were open to interstate travel. In Anniston, Alabama, whites burned one of the buses and attacked the riders. White mobs attacked the Freedom Riders in both Birmingham and Montgomery, Alabama. Kennedy was embarrassed by the public attention directed at the civil rights violations and at the violence.[15] Communists overseas used such negative publicity to emphasize the human rights problems abounding in the United States, and the timing could not have been worse. Kennedy was about to meet with Soviet premier Nikita Khrushchev.

Alabama government officials would not guarantee the safety of the Freedom Riders, so Kennedy sent six hundred federal marshals to stop the attacks on the riders. The Freedom Riders then continued on to Jackson, Mississippi, where officials arrested them for breaking a variety of local laws. These arrests ended the Freedom Rides, but attempts to desegregate the South continued. The fierce commitment of the Freedom Riders demonstrated to Americans—and to their president—how far civil rights supporters would go to reach their goals.

In June 1961, Kennedy had scheduled a summit meeting, or series of talks, with Khrushchev in Vienna, Austria. Kennedy felt these talks would provide him with an opportunity to rebuild his image as a statesman after the embarrassing fiasco at the Bay of Pigs.[16] On the way to Vienna, the president and first lady stopped in Paris,

France. Kennedy and French president Charles de Gaulle discussed nuclear weapons and the defense of Western Europe. The first lady, speaking fluent French, managed to charm both de Gaulle and the entire French nation. She received so much attention that Kennedy wryly noted at a news conference, "I do not think it entirely inappropriate for me to introduce myself. I am the man who accompanied Jacqueline Kennedy to Paris—and I have enjoyed it."[17] Both Kennedys delighted the Parisians with their youthful appearance and savoir faire.

Kennedy's meetings with Khrushchev took place in Vienna on June 3 and 4. Khrushchev treated the American president with visible contempt, as if Kennedy were too young and indecisive to be taken seriously. The two world leaders discussed mutual involvement in Laos and Vietnam. They agreed on the need for a neutral and independent government in Laos. Another topic was nuclear disarmament, or taking apart and getting rid of nuclear weapons. However, no agreement was reached. Khrushchev refused to allow United States or United Nations inspections of Soviet weapons sites. However, he did promise Kennedy that the Soviets would not resume nuclear testing unless the Americans did.

The two leaders strongly disagreed on whether changes should be made in the geographical division of Germany and Berlin. After World War II, the Western Allies (the United States, Great Britain, France) and their eastern ally, the USSR, had divided Germany into four zones of military occupation. Berlin, which was located within the Soviet zone, was also divided into four sectors. It soon became clear that the four powers would have difficulty governing Germany jointly, because the Western nations wanted to form a democracy, whereas the Soviet Union supported communism. As a result, West Germany, under the leadership of the United States, was formed from the three Western zones of military occupation. The Soviet Union responded by converting its zone into Communist East Germany. Ever since the end of World War II, Allied troops had remained in West Germany as a show of support against communism. As Cold War tensions increased, the United States increased its military presence in West Germany, as did the USSR in East Germany.

From that point on, discord increased regarding the governance of Berlin and access to the city. The three sectors of Berlin governed by the Western powers together formed the democratic section of West Berlin. The Soviet sector became Communist East Berlin. Between 1949 and

In June 1961, Kennedy meets in Vienna, Austria, with Soviet premier Nikita Khrushchev to discuss world affairs.

1961, 2.7 million people escaped communism by fleeing from East Germany to West Berlin.[18] Khrushchev was determined to stop the flow of refugees to the West. He also insisted that the West no longer had a right to have a presence in West Berlin because, in forming West Germany, the Allied powers had broken their postwar agreement to govern Germany together with the Soviets.

In making such statements, Khrushchev ignored the USSR's unwillingness to work with the Allies. He told Kennedy that within the next six months, he planned to sign a separate peace treaty with East Germany. It would require the Western nations to give up their occupation of West Berlin and remove the troops they had stationed there since the end of World War II. After signing this treaty, Khrushchev would block any further American access to Berlin. Kennedy refused to consider withdrawing American troops. He warned the Russian premier that, if necessary, he would use force if the United States were not allowed access to Berlin. Khrushchev insisted that he would fight back.

The president, sensing that the possibility of war was close, called for an increase in the size of military forces by more than two hundred thousand troops.[19] Reserve units of troops were also called up, and the tours of duty for regular troops were extended. Soon the number of United States military forces in West Germany was at full strength. If necessary, the president was prepared to go to war over the issue of access to Berlin. The thought of war was such a realistic possibility that Kennedy also stressed the need for Americans at home to build bomb shelters, or reinforced underground concrete bunkers. If a bombing attack were imminent, people could seek safety in these shelters, which stored enough food, bottled water, and other survival supplies for a long siege.

On August 13, 1961, tensions increased when East German troops set up roadblocks and barbed wire around East Berlin. A few days later, construction of a concrete wall began. East German president Walter Ulbricht, with Khrushchev's support, had decided to halt the flow of refugees escaping from East to West Berlin. The East Germans' actions caught Kennedy by surprise while he was vacationing in Hyannis Port. Kennedy sent a protest to Moscow, the capital of the USSR. However, some critics later remarked that the United States should have acted more forcefully. American troops stationed in West Germany could easily have knocked down the Berlin Wall.[20] The wall soon became the physical symbol of what had already become known as the Iron Curtain, the ideological boundary dividing Eastern and Western Europe, communism and democracy.

West Berlin mayor Willy Brandt appealed to Kennedy for help. The president was determined to show Khrushchev that the West intended to defend its presence in West Berlin. Kennedy decided to send fifteen hundred American soldiers to West Berlin. The city was located one hundred ten miles inside of East Germany. To reach West Berlin from West Germany, people had to travel along the autobahn, or superhighway, from Helmstedt, West Germany, through East Germany.[21] The president wondered whether Soviet troops would stop the progress of the American convoy at any point along the way. Kennedy was relieved when the troops arrived safely in West Berlin to an enthusiastic welcome.

Kennedy's handling of the tense situation showed not

only an aggressive stance but also consideration of his serious responsibilities in preventing war. However, the immediate threat of war was over—for a time.

The USSR continued to strike an aggressive posture. On August 30, despite promises Khrushchev had made in Vienna, the Soviets announced that they would resume testing nuclear weapons. Kennedy then announced that the United States, too, would resume its testing.

The year 1961 ended on a sad personal note for the president. His seventy-three-year-old father suffered a severe stroke. This is a rupture or blood clot in an artery of the brain. The stroke paralyzed the right side of Joe Kennedy's body. Although he lost the ability to speak, his mind remained intact. Jack Kennedy remarked, "Even if my Dad had only ten percent of his brain working, I'd still feel he had more sense than anyone else."[22] The elder Kennedy's inability to move and communicate left him angry and frustrated. Kennedy visited him regularly on weekends. Now that his father could no longer give him advice, Jack treasured his brother Bobby's political guidance more than ever.[23] Jack Kennedy had lost his father's advice—but at least he was free from his father's controlling power.[24]

9

CHALLENGES AND SUCCESSES

I n John F. Kennedy's second year as president, the United States space program reached another milestone. On February 2, 1962, John Glenn became a hero when he orbited the earth three times.

The year 1962 brought increased American involvement in the war in Vietnam. Vietnam, a former French colony, had been divided into north and south sectors in 1952. North Vietnam was supported by Communists, whereas South Vietnam's democratic government was being backed by the United States. At the time, Communist intervention in any nation was considered a threat to the security of the United States. American policy was based on the "domino theory," or the fear that if one nation fell to communism, others around it would soon fall, too.

President Kennedy, like his predecessor Dwight D. Eisenhower, believed in the domino theory. In 1960, the

Communist National Liberation Front (NLF) with its North Vietnamese guerrilla fighters called the Vietcong began to attack South Vietnamese cities and villages. Kennedy hoped that the South Vietnamese Army could fight off the Vietcong with United States support. He increased the number of American military advisers to South Vietnam from 948 in November 1961 to 11,000 by the end of 1962. These advisers were sent without the knowledge of the American public—and their role gradually changed from mere "advising" to one involving combat. In February 1962, Kennedy publicly admitted that American troops were "firing back" at the Vietcong to protect themselves.[1]

On the domestic front, the steel industry challenged Kennedy's authority. On March 31, 1962, industry leaders and the United Steelworkers, an organized labor union, agreed to freeze industry wages for a year. Kennedy considered the agreed upon contract a victory because a steelworkers' strike would have threatened the nation's economy. However, on April 10, the United States Steel Corporation abruptly announced an increase of six dollars a ton in the price of steel. Traditionally, the pay scale established by United States Steel was soon followed by the other eleven major steel companies.[2] Kennedy accused United States Steel of ignoring what was best for the nation's economic health.[3] Five more steel companies announced price hikes identical to that of United States Steel. The administration ordered the FBI to investigate whether or not steel executives had followed illegal practices. By April 13, the steel companies rolled back their price increases, giving Kennedy a triumph over the powerful steel industry.

By September 1962, Kennedy had succeeded in having

some legislation passed. Congress supported the United States Arms Control and Disarmament Agency. Congress also passed increases in Social Security benefits and raised the minimum wage to $1.25 per hour. The Housing Act supplied much-needed funds for redevelopment. However, Congress passed only 44.3 percent of Kennedy's proposed legislation in 1962.[4]

That same month, Kennedy reached a turning point in his mostly detached position on civil rights.[5] James Meredith, a twenty-nine-year-old African American, attempted to enroll in the all-white University of Mississippi at Oxford. To avoid any violence, federal marshals escorted Meredith onto the "Ole Miss" campus on September 25. However, Mississippi governor Ross Barnett refused to register Meredith. Kennedy hoped to resolve the situation by negotiation instead of by calling out federal troops. When a court order directed Barnett to allow Meredith to register, Barnett agreed to have Meredith register secretly in Jackson, Mississippi, the state capital, to draw attention away from Oxford. When two federal officials brought Meredith to Jackson, however, Barnett refused to let him register. Attorney General Robert Kennedy worked out a new agreement in which Barnett promised to let Meredith register on the Oxford campus under the protection of state police. When this agreement was reached, President Kennedy then broadcast over national television that Meredith had indeed registered. In fact, Barnett broke this promise, too, and refused to allow Meredith to enroll, and a riot broke out on campus. Hundreds, including 166 United States marshals, were injured in the rioting. A French news reporter was shot in the back, and a construction worker, who was watching the rioting, was accidentally shot in the head. Kennedy sent federal troops to restore order. On October 1, 1962, Meredith, with a bodyguard of six federal marshals and Army troops waiting in trucks, was finally registered as a student. The president's popularity rating rose as a result of his firm leadership in restoring order.[6]

Just sixteen days later, Kennedy was faced with the biggest single political showdown of his career. It lasted for thirteen days and threatened to cause nuclear war. It was called the Cuban Missile Crisis.

On October 16, American U-2 spy planes flying over Cuba brought back photos showing that several Soviet missile-launching sites were under construction on the island. These were offensive weapons, which when completed would be fired without warning, not necessarily in response to an attack. Such missiles could reach and destroy major American cities. They could also destroy United States military bases and the space launch site at Cape Canaveral, Florida. The Soviets claimed that they had sent Cuba only technical advisers and defensive weapons.[7] The photographs proved that the Soviets had lied.

Kennedy immediately created an advisory committee, the Executive Committee of the National Security Council (ExComm). ExComm was made up of the president's closest advisers. It included Attorney General Robert Kennedy, three other Cabinet members, members of the military and the CIA, and state department officials. ExComm's job was to recommend a solution to this Cuban Missile Crisis. ExComm considered four alternatives: bombing Cuba; invading by land; blockading, or encircling, the island with ships; or working with the United Nations to negotiate a settlement.

On October 20, after careful consideration of all the alternatives, the committee recommended a naval defensive quarantine.[8] This measure was aimed at keeping Soviet ships from delivering more weapons and supplies to Cuba. It meant that a ring of United States Navy ships would surround Cuba. Any foreign vessels suspected of carrying weapons and missile parts would be stopped and turned back. A defensive quarantine is similar to a blockade. However, a blockade is considered an act of war. A quarantine would allow the Kennedy administration to send a strong signal, but it would stop short of war. It would also offer an "out," or a way to save face, to Soviet premier Khrushchev. He could avoid confrontation by ordering his ships to turn back.[9] However, it would take the United States Navy time to get its vessels into position

The Executive Committee of the National Security Council (ExComm) meets in the White House in October 1962 to find a solution to the Cuban Missile Crisis.

to form the quarantine. In the meantime, the Soviet missiles could become fully operational.

Quickly, the United States military was placed on alert, in case the president decided to choose a different option, a strong military action such as bombing Cuba or invading by land. Five hundred fifty B-52 aircraft carrying nuclear bombs were sent circling in the air near Cuba, waiting for a signal from the president to move in and drop their bombs over the island. More than one hundred thousand troops were sent to Florida in readiness for a possible land invasion. The Navy already had more than one hundred eighty ships in the water near Cuba because of a previously planned training exercise.

The final decision was up to the president. If nothing were done, the world would soon know that John F. Kennedy had allowed Nikita Khrushchev to build nuclear weapons "in the United States' own backyard."[10] He would appear powerless and cowardly. Kennedy decided he would take action by putting the quarantine in place.

Such a strong step, however, might be viewed as an act of aggression by the allies of the United States. Before starting the quarantine, special meetings were scheduled with the leaders of West Germany, Great Britain, Canada, and France to inform them of the plan. All these leaders supported President Kennedy's decision. Unanimous support also came from the Organization of American States (OAS), made up of nations of the Western Hemisphere.

Congressional leaders were also informed of the president's proposed action. Many of them told Kennedy they thought he should take stronger action, such as a military attack or an invasion.[11] Kennedy explained that he intended to fully guard the United States' security, but that he believed stronger military action should not be taken right away.[12]

On October 22, 1962, at 7:00 P.M., President Kennedy broadcast his decision worldwide. He announced that the United States planned "a quarantine of offensive military equipment under shipment to Cuba."[13] United States Navy ships would form a ring, or quarantine, five hundred miles away from Cuban shores. Only ships carrying ordinary cargo such as food or oil, not weapons, would be allowed through the quarantine. Kennedy called on Khrushchev to withdraw all weapons already in Cuba and to stop the preparation of missile sites there. The president appealed to the Soviet premier to stop his "reckless and provocative threat to world peace and to stable relations between our two nations."[14] Kennedy emphasized, ". . . the greatest danger of all would be to do nothing. . . . Our goal is not the victory of might, but the vindication of right—not peace at the expense of freedom, but both peace *and* freedom. . . ."[15]

According to a Gallup opinion poll taken the next day, 84 percent of Americans backed the president in his choice of using the quarantine.[16] Kennedy's seventeen-minute radio and television message had put the Soviets and the Cubans on alert that the quarantine would be merely an initial step. The United States would take stronger military action if the Soviet missiles were not removed from Cuba.

The quarantine would not go into effect until 10:00 A.M. on Wednesday, October 24. This delay allowed the Soviets two days to withdraw their ships from the area. Sixteen American destroyers, three cruisers, an antisubmarine aircraft carrier, and more than one hundred fifty additional ships formed the Navy quarantine ring around Cuba.[17] Tensions were high at the White House. "I guess this is the week I earn my salary," Kennedy commented to one of his aides.[18] Within a few minutes after the start of the quarantine, the six Soviet ships nearest the edge of the quarantine ring had stopped or turned back.

The next day, the Soviet oil tanker *Bucharest* was allowed past the United States ships, because it was not carrying any weapons. Early in the morning on Friday, October 26, United States Navy officers boarded their first foreign ship. By coincidence, these officers were from the destroyer *Joseph P. Kennedy, Jr.*, named after Kennedy's older brother, who had died during World War II. The president had carefully chosen the first foreign ship they would board.[19] It was the *Marucla*, a Lebanese freighter, owned by Panama, operating under a Soviet charter. Since it was not actually owned by the Soviets, boarding it did not represent a direct challenge to their authority. This action, according to Robert Kennedy, gave Khrushchev more time to respond to the American position, yet it showed clearly that the United States "meant business."[20] The Navy found no missiles aboard, so the *Marucla* was allowed past the American vessels.

Later on October 26, Khrushchev sent the first of two letters to the United States government. He promised that no more weapons would be sent to Cuba and that those already within Cuba's territory would be withdrawn or destroyed. In return, he asked that the United States government recall its fleet and not attack Cuba.

On the following day, however, two threatening situations occurred. Another letter arrived from Khrushchev. It demanded that the United States remove its Jupiter missiles from Turkey. The missiles were part of the North Atlantic Treaty Organization (NATO) defense system. America's

NATO allies, Great Britain, France, and Turkey, had asked the United States to install these missiles to protect Europe from any aggression by Soviet Russia.

Also on October 27, an American U-2 spy plane was shot down over Cuba, killing the pilot. Previously, President Kennedy and ExComm had decided to attack Cuba with missiles if any American spy planes were shot down. The president was now under immense pressure to strike back, but he wanted to make sure that the U-2 had not been shot down accidentally.[21]

President Kennedy sent his brother Bobby to meet with Ambassador Dobrynin from the USSR in the attorney general's office in the Justice Department. Bobby Kennedy told Dobrynin that the United States accepted Khrushchev's offer to remove the Soviet missiles from Cuba. However, he added, the United States refused to remove its Jupiter missiles from Turkey without the approval of NATO. Bobby Kennedy made it clear to Dobrynin that the United States did plan to remove its Jupiter missiles at a later time. He insisted that, within twenty-four hours, Khrushchev respond to the American conditions: that the Soviets stop work on the Cuban missile bases and that they promise to deactivate their offensive missiles there, or else the United States would take stronger military action.[22]

While Americans slept, Premier Khrushchev and his advisers met. On Sunday, October 28, Moscow radio broadcast the news that Nikita Khrushchev had accepted the United States' offer.

Soviet leaders had underrated the United States' ability to detect the presence of their missiles. They did not think President Kennedy would respond to this discovery so quickly and with such firmness. Khrushchev was a strong-willed leader who had formed an erroneous first impression that Kennedy was an inexperienced young leader.[23] He had underestimated the president's courage under difficult circumstances.

The United States' prestige—and the reputation of its president—went sky-high after the Cuban Missile Crisis. Kennedy's decisions revealed his deep concern about the possibility of nuclear war. During the crisis, he told aide Dave Powers, "I keep thinking about the children whose lives would be wiped out."[24]

The world saw the American president as cool under pressure. After the missile crisis, British prime minister Harold Macmillan said, "If Kennedy never did another thing, he assured his place in history."[25]

Kennedy closed out the year with a relaxed television news interview on December 17, 1962. "After Two Years— A Conversation with the President" boosted his public appeal. The happy news that the Kennedys were expecting another baby added to the president's popularity and to his image as a devoted family man.

The first major civil rights activity of 1963 occurred in Birmingham, Alabama. Dr. Martin Luther King, Jr., started a protest campaign in April. It included street marches and sit-ins at downtown stores. On Friday, April 12, King was jailed for demonstrating. He was released a week later. President Kennedy used negotiators to get the white and African-American leaders to work together. The white leadership promised to desegregate restaurants and lunch counters within ninety days. Many businesses made more and better jobs available for African Americans. The events at Birmingham moved the civil rights movement to the national forefront.

Kennedy also continued to take a global leadership role. On June 10, he gave a moving speech on foreign policy at American University in Washington, D.C. He pledged to work toward peace with America's enemies like the USSR. In the Soviet Union, for the first time, the government allowed citizens to listen to the speech. Kennedy and his advisers speculated that perhaps this was a sign that the Soviets were indicating a willingness to deal constructively with Americans.

Late that same day, a Buddhist monk burned himself to death in the middle of a busy intersection in the South Vietnamese capital, Saigon. His action protested the corrupt government of South Vietnamese president Ngo Dinh Diem. Diem, a puppet, or powerless figurehead, of the United States government, was a Catholic aristocrat ruling what was mainly a country of Buddhist peasants. Diem barricaded the city's Buddhist pagodas in response to the monk's suicide. He would allow no demonstrations against his government.

The following day another domestic civil rights crisis erupted. Two African Americans, Vivian Malone and James Hood, had been admitted to the University of Alabama. However, Alabama's governor, George Wallace, refused to allow them to register. Only five months before, in his inaugural address, Wallace had pledged to keep the state segregated forever,[26] but university officials agreed to accept a court order to admit the students. Wallace overruled the officials by appointing himself the university's temporary registrar. In response, President Kennedy took control of the five hundred members of the Alabama

National Guard who were drilling on the University of Alabama campus. Kennedy was prepared to use force to make sure that Malone and Hood were registered. When Wallace was informed of Kennedy's action, Vivian Malone and James Hood were allowed to register as students.

That evening, President Kennedy spoke about civil rights on national television. With his actions regarding the students at the University of Alabama, Kennedy had taken a definite step toward a strong commitment to action on civil rights. He asked Congress to enact legislation to end segregation in public education, as well as in hotels, restaurants, and other public facilities. He also called for Congress to protect the rights of African Americans to vote.

On June 19, he spoke to Congress about the struggle for civil rights for African Americans. He emphasized the need to eliminate violence, like the attacks on the Freedom Riders and James Meredith. Kennedy also urged passage of legislation to eliminate racial discrimination.

On June 22, 1963, Kennedy flew to Europe for a ten-day tour. He planned to visit Ireland, England, Italy, and West Berlin. The visit to Ireland was a vacation. In England, Kennedy and British prime minister Harold Macmillan agreed to push for a nuclear test ban agreement with Moscow. In Italy, Kennedy talked with the new pope, Paul VI, about world peace.

Cheering crowds greeted Kennedy in West Berlin. Kennedy gave a speech explaining that although some people felt it was possible to work with Communists, the example of Berlin proved that this was untrue. He said, "Freedom has many difficulties and democracy is not perfect, but we have never had to put a wall up to keep our people in," as had been the case in East Germany.[27] He closed by saying, "All free men, wherever they may live, are citizens of Berlin, and therefore, as a free man, I take pride in the words '*Ich bin ein Berliner* [I am a Berliner].'"[28]

On July 15, talks opened in Moscow on the subject of banning nuclear testing. The United States, the Soviet Union, and Great Britain participated. These nations agreed to forbid testing nuclear devices in outer space, the atmosphere, and the oceans. The ban was a huge step toward peaceful relations between the United States and the Soviet Union. Less than a year before, these two nations had nearly gone to war over Cuba.

Because of her advanced pregnancy, Jackie stayed in

On June 26, 1963, Kennedy appears in Berlin with Otto Bach (right) of the West Berlin House of Representatives. In his speech, Kennedy delivers his famous line, "Ich bin ein Berliner," ("I am a Berliner").

Washington during Jack's summer travels. On August 7, 1963, Patrick Bouvier Kennedy was born five and one-half weeks prematurely. Weighing only four pounds, the infant had a severe breathing problem. He was immediately moved to a Boston hospital where he could receive special care. The president visited him four times that day. Sadly, Patrick was too small and weak to recover. He died on August 9, 1963.

Both parents were deeply distressed. The president wept openly. Jackie later said, "He felt the loss of the baby . . . as much as I did."[29] However, the baby's death brought the couple closer.[30] The president reached out to his wife to comfort her and to receive comfort himself.

African-American leader Martin Luther King, Jr., led a march on Washington, D.C., on August 28, 1963. His goal was to draw attention to the need for more civil rights legislation. The civil rights demonstration was the largest one in American history. A crowd of two hundred thirty thousand participated—peacefully. King stood before the Lincoln Memorial and gave this now famous speech:

> I have a dream that one day . . . when we let freedom ring, when we let it ring from every village and every hamlet . . . we will be able to speed up that day when all God's children, black men and white men, Jews and Gentiles, Protestants and Catholics, will be able to join in the words of that old Negro spiritual "Free at last! Free at last! Thank God almighty, we are free at last!"[31]

After the march, Kennedy met with African-American leaders. They discussed ways to increase the chances of passing civil rights laws.

By that fall, the Kennedy administration had a major civil rights bill before Congress. Opinion polls showed that most Americans supported the bill, although strong pockets of resistance remained in parts of the nation. The Civil Rights Act of 1964 finally passed after Kennedy's death. It guaranteed African Americans the right to be served in public places and to seek a job without the fear of racial discrimination. It also guaranteed the desegregation of public schools, forcing them to offer admission to all races.

By November 1963, the United States had over sixteen thousand advisers in South Vietnam. That same month, the South Vietnamese government of President Diem was overthrown. Military generals under the leadership of General Duong Van Minh, a Buddhist who had long opposed the Catholic president Diem, took control. The United States had assured the South Vietnamese military that it would not oppose its coup, or overthrow, of Diem's government.[32] Diem was assassinated in the takeover. Kennedy considered what to do next. He remained strongly committed to stopping the spread of communism anywhere in the world. His brother Bobby said, "The President felt that he had a strong, overwhelming reason for being in Vietnam and that we should win the war in Vietnam."[33] Yet on other occasions, Kennedy had expressed doubts about the level of United States commitment necessary in Southeast Asia.[34] Still, on November 8, 1963, the United States formally recognized the new, military government of South Vietnam.

Meanwhile, Kennedy began planning his race for a second term as president. The election was only a year away.

10

ASSASSINATION AFTERMATH

On November 22, 1963, before much progress was made on the new campaign, President John F. Kennedy was assassinated. Ninety-nine minutes after Kennedy's death, Lyndon Baines Johnson, Kennedy's vice-president, was sworn in as the thirty-sixth president of the United States. It was vitally important for the nation's confidence to know that a new leader had taken quick control. Jackie Kennedy and Johnson's wife, Lady Bird, flanked the new president as he took the oath of office aboard the presidential jet, *Air Force One*, still sitting in the Dallas airport. Then the plane took off for Washington, D.C. No one yet knew why President Kennedy had been assassinated or who had committed this tragic act. Thus, it was important to make sure that President and Mrs. Johnson and the former first lady were moved away from the assassination site as quickly as possible.

With them on board *Air Force One* was President

Kennedy's vice-president, Lyndon B. Johnson, takes the presidential oath of office aboard Air Force One. *Jacqueline Kennedy (far right) looks on.*

Kennedy's casket. Jackie Kennedy sat in the rear of the plane near her slain husband's body. Although she was still in shock, she talked with Kennedy aides, recalling favorite memories about her husband. She still wore the once perfect pink suit, now stained with her husband's blood, and her grief was apparent.

A few hours after Kennedy's assassination in Dallas, police officers arrested a suspect in the president's murder. Lee Harvey Oswald, a twenty-four-year-old former United States Marine, worked at the Texas School Book Depository building. On the sixth floor of the depository, which faced out onto Dealey Plaza and provided an ideal view of the president's motorcade, officers had discovered a rifle. It was later identified as Oswald's. Right after the shootings, a witness had spotted a rifle being quickly withdrawn from a sixth-floor window. Police officers gathered all the depository employees to question them. Oswald was missing. Police broadcast his description. A police officer, John D. Tippit, stopped a man fitting this description. The suspect, who turned out to be Oswald, shot and killed Officer Tippit, then ran away. Oswald was soon arrested in a movie theater, where he was hiding. The Dallas police charged him with killing both the president and Officer Tippit, and he was taken to the Dallas city jail to be held for questioning.

As it later turned out, Oswald had a history of problems with authority. He had been court-martialed, or given a military trial, for talking back to his superior officer in the Marines. Oswald had also had difficulty holding a job. His interest in communism looked suspicious to the police. In 1959, after his discharge from the Marines, Oswald had moved to the Soviet Union to live. This looked suspicious, too. However, the Soviets would not grant him citizenship, and in 1962, Oswald returned to the United States with his Russian-born wife, Marina, and their daughter.

Back in the capital, Jackie Kennedy had already begun planning a dignified funeral for her husband. His casket was laid in state in the East Room of the White House. She had chosen this room specifically because President Abraham Lincoln's casket had also lain there after an assassin's bullet had killed him in 1865. The room was hung with black curtains, and an American flag was ceremoniously draped across the casket, just like Lincoln's.

On the morning of November 24, Jackie and Bobby

In this picture taken in March 1963, Lee Harvey Oswald poses holding the same rifle that he was later accused of using to shoot President Kennedy.

Kennedy paid a solemn visit to the president's coffin. Inside, they placed letters written by Jackie and Caroline, and doodles from John-John, who was too young to really write. Jackie also added a pair of gold cuff links and an ivory carving with the presidential seal on it. Bobby put in the PT-109 tie clip that his brother had given him.

Soon after this visit, the casket was taken outside and placed on a two-wheeled gun carriage, or caisson, the same one that had carried President Franklin D. Roosevelt's casket for his funeral procession in 1945. Kennedy's caisson was pulled by a team of gray horses, and a riderless black stallion named Black Jack followed behind. A pair of black boots stood reversed in the stirrups. They represented the warrior who would never ride again. A slow, mournful procession made its way up

Dignitaries from around the world pay their last respects to the slain young American leader whose casket lies in state in the Rotunda of the Capitol.

Pennsylvania Avenue. Crowds lined the route, just as they had in Dallas two days before, but now the waving and cheering had given way to weeping and shock. When the procession reached the Capitol, the casket was carried upstairs and placed in the Rotunda.

On the same day, November 24, the investigation into President Kennedy's assassination experienced a huge setback when Oswald himself was murdered. Live television cameras were broadcasting his transfer from the Dallas city jail to the county jail. Horrified viewers across the nation watched this live broadcast as Dallas nightclub owner Jack Ruby stepped out of the crowd of observers and reporters. In a second, he stuck his gun into Oswald's ribs and shot him down. Later, Ruby said that he did it to protect Jackie Kennedy from suffering through Oswald's murder trial.[1] Now that Oswald was dead, police and government officials would never know for certain whether or not Oswald had actually shot the president. In 1964, Ruby was sentenced to death for murdering Oswald; however, this verdict was overturned because the trial was ruled unfair. Ruby died of cancer in 1967, still in jail awaiting a new trial.

The day after Oswald's death, John F. Kennedy's funeral took place at St. Matthew's Cathedral in Washington. After the service, the casket was carried back to the caisson for the trip to the cemetery. Millions of viewers around the world watched the solemn procession on television. As the gun carriage carrying his father passed the spot where the Kennedy family was gathered, John F. Kennedy, Jr., saluted. It was his third birthday.

President Kennedy was laid to rest in Arlington National Cemetery in Virginia. His wife had arranged for

On November 24, as Lee Harvey Oswald (second from left) is about to be transferred from the Dallas city jail, nightclub owner Jack Ruby (center, bottom) pulls out a gun. Seconds later, Ruby shoots Oswald dead.

his grave to be marked by an eternal flame, one that never burns out.

The new president, Lyndon B. Johnson, moved quickly to examine the causes of President Kennedy's death. He hoped to eliminate growing fears that there had been a plot, or conspiracy, against the government. Johnson formed a special commission on November 29, 1963, to look into the facts of the case and to come to a conclusion about who was responsible for this national tragedy. Johnson appointed Earl Warren, Chief Justice of the Supreme Court, as chairman of the commission, which bore Warren's name. Ten months later, the Warren Commission issued its findings, *The Warren Report*. It concluded that Lee Harvey Oswald had killed both President Kennedy and Officer Tippet. The Warren Commission found no evidence that anyone other than Oswald had planned or carried out the assassination.[2] It concluded that only three shots were fired at the president. They were supposedly fired from the direction of behind and somewhat above the president's car. Thus, the Warren Commission believed the shots were fired from the textbook depository building.

The Warren Report did not stop the worldwide speculation about causes and conspiracies involving the president's assassination. Although many witnesses claimed to have heard more than three shots, only three cartridges, or metal casings of a bullet, were recovered. The Warren Commission's reasoning went like this: One bullet went all the way through Kennedy's body and hit Governor Connally. Another bullet hit the president's head, lodging inside his skull, and killed him. The third bullet, which missed hitting either Kennedy or Connally, hit a

The Warren Commission report includes this photograph, showing a mock-up of the presidential limousine lined up in the assassin's rifle scope.

curb on the south side of Main Street. Several witnesses had seen sparks and smoke, evidence that a bullet had struck the curbing.

To account for only three bullets being fired, with one single bullet causing damage to both Kennedy and Connolly as the Commission concluded, its theory of what happened became known as the "single" or "magic" bullet theory.[3] Governor Connally suffered wounds in the back, ribs, wrist, and thigh. Fragments from the so-called magic bullet were removed from his body during surgery on November 22, 1963. The rest of the slug, in relatively good condition, was found on his hospital stretcher that day. Critics questioned the commission's explanation of how this bullet had passed first through Kennedy's throat, into Governor Connally's back, through Connally's rib cage, into his wrist, and then finally back into his thigh, without suffering noticeable damage. They also questioned whether or not the angle of such a shot would have been possible from the depository building's sixth-floor window.

By 1966, *Life* magazine called for a new investigation of Kennedy's assassination. The magazine had obtained a copy of an eight-millimeter home movie of the assassination taken by a bystander named Abraham Zapruder. The magazine arranged a special screening for Governor Connally. After viewing the film, Connally was even more certain than ever that he had been hit by a separate bullet, not the so-called magic bullet.[4] Up until his death on June 15, 1993, Connally maintained that Kennedy had been hit by the first and third bullets fired, while he had been hit by the sniper's second shot.[5] When Connally heard the first shot, he said he had time to turn and look over both his right and left shoulders before he knew he had been hit by a bullet.[6] Such a lapse of time indicated to the governor that he had been struck by a different bullet than any that had hit the president. However, if Connally had been hit by a different bullet, who shot the bullet that left the mark on the Main Street curb?

Critics stated that it was impossible for Oswald to have fired all three bullets in such rapid succession from the rifle recovered on the sixth floor of the depository.[7] Yet the commission reached this conclusion, based on tests that were not fully disclosed in *The Warren Report*. The commission used three master marksmen to test their conclusion.

They were allowed to shoot at stationary target areas representing the entire upper portion of a man's body, even though Oswald, or whoever had shot the president, was aiming at a moving target of just the president's head and neck. Therefore, the test conditions and the assassination situation were not alike.

It seemed as if either someone else must have done the shooting or another person or persons had assisted Oswald. Many Americans seemed to support this conclusion, since in 1966, a Gallup poll showed that only 39 percent believed that Oswald had acted on his own and killed the president.[8]

Conflicts in the medical evidence also caused doubts. The Warren Commission had never even seen the X rays and photographs taken at the president's autopsy performed at Bethesda Naval Hospital. An autopsy is a detailed medical examination to determine the cause of a person's death. Several of the original autopsy X rays are now missing or appear to have been changed.[9] Some of the original autopsy photos have also disappeared.[10] The autopsy report does not match the photographs and X rays of the body.[11] Kennedy's brain, which was analyzed during the autopsy, somehow disappeared between April 1965 and October 1966.[12]

Medical testimony of the doctors involved in the case caused further confusion. Physicians who treated Kennedy at Parkland Hospital maintained that the president's wounds indicated that he seemed to have been shot from the front, not the rear, as the Warren Commission concluded.[13] Yet Secret Service agents told these doctors to state that the president's wounds showed he had been shot from the rear.[14] The Parkland Hospital physicians also noted that the wounds they observed on the president's body did not match those shown in autopsy photographs.[15] Commander James J. Humes, who had conducted the president's autopsy, said he was given orders not to talk about the procedure.[16] To many Americans, these discrepancies and lack of candor on the part of government officials seemed to indicate that facts about the assassination were being concealed.

Critics also accused the Warren Commission of failing to question all witnesses and of ignoring some of the evidence. The report disregarded the testimony of witnesses who believed that an assassin had fired from the grassy knoll area north of Elm Street. These witnesses claim to have seen smoke or steam near the trees at the top of the knoll.[17] Although the Warren Commission concluded that Oswald, and Oswald alone, was the assassin, many people believe facts were made to fit this conclusion.

Finally, in 1979, the House Select Committee on Assassinations, appointed by the House in 1976, reexamined the details of the assassination. It reached a conclusion that differed from that of the Warren Commission: Probably more than one person was involved in the president's murder.[18] The committee's acoustics, or sound, experts listened to police radio recordings made during the assassination. The committee concluded that shots had come from two directions. One area was the book depository. However, they felt a rifle had also been fired from the area of the grassy knoll in front of the president.[19] The congressional committee admitted it could not identify any other gunman or the nature of any conspiracy, or secret plot, to murder the president.

In December 1991, the release of Oliver Stone's movie

⭐ **SOURCE DOCUMENT** ⭐

ATTOPSY DESC   (1-63)

AUTOPSY

NMS # A **63 # 27 2** DATE *11-22-63* HR. STARTED_____ HR.COMPLETED_____

NAME: _____ RANK/RATE _____

DATE/HOUR EXPIRED:_____ WARD _____ DIAGNOSIS _____

PHYSICAL DESCRIPTION: RACE: _____ Obtain following on babies only:
                                    Color
Height_____in. Weight_____lb. Hair_____   Crown-rump_____ in.
                                             Crown-heel_____ in.
Color eyes_____ Pupils:Rt_____mm, Lb.____mm Circumference:
WEIGHTS: (Grams, unless otherwise specified) Head_____in. Chest_____in.
                                             Abd._____in.

LUNG, RT. ~~390~~ 320   KIDNEY, RT. *150*   ADRENALS, RT. _____

LUNG, LT. ~~290~~ 290   KIDNEY, LT. *140*   ADRENALS, LT. _____

BRAIN _____   LIVER *650*   PANCREAS _____

SPLEEN *90*   HEART *360*   THYROID _____ *1*

THYMUS _____   TESTIS _____ OVARY _____

HEART MEASUREMENTS: A *7.5* cm. P *7* cm. T *12* cm. M *10* dm.

                    LVM *1.5* cm. RVM *.4* cm.

NOTES:

These drawings indicating the location and size of President Kennedy's gunshot wounds were part of the official report made at Kennedy's autopsy.

JFK prompted a renewal of interest in the assassination. Stone said he made the film to "remind people how much our nation and our world lost when President Kennedy died."[20] He, too, concluded that Oswald did not act alone in murdering the president. In addition, Stone believed that the CIA, other government agencies, and perhaps even President Lyndon Johnson might have been involved.[21] Stone based his film on an independent investigation conducted after the assassination by District Attorney Jim Garrison from New Orleans. After years of research, Garrison believed that a conspiracy was behind the assassination.[22] Garrison felt the key planners were agents of the CIA.[23]

The film received both criticism and praise. However, it did have an important result. Its publicity caused the public to put pressure on Congress for new information. In 1992, Congress passed the Assassination Materials Disclosure Act. A presidential panel formed to examine previously classified materials. The first documents were released in August 1993. An estimated 3 million documents will end up in the National Archives. Now researchers, historians, and the general public will be able to study materials that had been kept secret for almost twenty years.

Five main theories persist about who might have conspired to kill the president:

> *Soviet or Cuban Communists:* Evidence for this theory was based on longtime Soviet boasts that they would destroy the United States. The Soviets may also have resented Kennedy's success during the Cuban Missile Crisis. Fidel Castro also

had a motive to kill the president. Through his own intelligence sources, the Cuban leader had learned that the CIA was plotting to assassinate him. Lee Harvey Oswald's membership in the pro-Castro Fair Play for Cuba Committee gave him a possible connection to Cuban Communists.

Cuban exiles: They may have plotted to kill Kennedy because of his failure to oust Castro during the Bay of Pigs invasion.

Organized crime: John and Robert Kennedy had both aggressively prosecuted organized crime groups, also known as the Mafia or the Mob. The president had also tried to have reputed New Orleans Mafia chief Carlos Marcello deported. Both Lee Harvey Oswald and Jack Ruby had possible Mafia connections. Oswald had spent time in New Orleans, where he was friendly with Mob associates.[24] Jack Ruby had several Mafia friends, including Carlos Marcello and Florida chief Santos Trafficante. A Chicago native, Ruby had served as a runner, or messenger, for mobster Al Capone. Because Ruby was experiencing severe financial problems, he may have accepted a Mafia contract to kill Oswald.

The CIA: Individual agents, strongly opposed to Castro, may have planned the assassination. They may have been embarrassed by their failure in planning the Bay of Pigs invasion. As a result, they may have feared that Kennedy would take away some of their power. Or they may have viewed the president's stand on communism as too soft.

Racist groups: Individuals opposed to Kennedy's stand on improving civil rights for African Americans might have planned his death.

Is one of these conspiracy theories correct? Or did lone gunman Lee Harvey Oswald kill John F. Kennedy as the Warren Commission concluded? Clearly the commission did not keep an open mind during its investigation. However, even today it seems that Oswald must have had at least some involvement with the assassination. It was his rifle found on the sixth floor of the book depository. He acted guilty in fleeing from the police and in murdering Officer Tippit.

He may have acted on his own. Or he may have been paid or had help from some other source. We may never know the truth of what really happened on that fateful day in 1963.

11

LEGACY

According to Ted Sorensen, one of Kennedy's speechwriters, Kennedy matured as a politician and as an individual during his years in office.[1] His experiences with personal tragedy and illness caused this growth. He developed both a desire to enjoy the world and a desire to improve it.

The world responded warmly to him. Memorials exist in more than two dozen West German cities. A Dublin concert hall is named after him. In Istanbul, Turkey, the Kennedy Forest attracts many visitors.

In the United States, five major sites memorialize its young leader. One is the John F. Kennedy Library and Museum just outside Boston, Massachusetts. His birthplace in Brookline, Massachusetts, is a national historic site. Kennedy's grave at Arlington National Cemetery in Virginia is a popular and moving tourist attraction. The Sixth Floor

Museum is housed on the actual sixth floor of the old Texas School Book Depository building in Dallas. It provides factual information about the president's death. Two blocks east of Dealey Plaza in Dallas is the John F. Kennedy Memorial. It is a cenotaph, or open tomb. Crowds gather there every year on the anniversary of the president's death.

In international affairs, Kennedy was committed to anticommunism and an aggressive foreign policy. Professor James N. Giglio of Southwest Missouri State University concluded that Kennedy's record was excellent as a crisis manager, but it was less effective in preventing crises from developing.[2] In particular, Kennedy demonstrated strong leadership during the Cuban Missile Crisis and the building of the Berlin Wall. Solving the Missile Crisis led to better Soviet-American relations. Within a year, a "hot line," or direct telephone line always ready for communication, was established between the capitals of both nations. Kennedy biographer Thomas C. Reeves, who was critical of Kennedy's character and its negative impact on his ability to make decisions, found that the president's handling of the Berlin crisis merited high praise: Kennedy's "defense of free world rights was morally defensible, effective, and highly popular."[3]

However, Kennedy made a poor choice to go ahead with the Bay of Pigs invasion in Cuba. Senator William Fulbright of Arkansas, chairman of the Foreign Relations Committee in 1961, criticized Kennedy for authorizing the invasion. Fulbright considered the project to be poorly thought out, as well as in violation of several international agreements and America's own federal laws against invading another nation.[4] Still, Kennedy accepted total responsibility for his choice.

Kennedy's focus on defeating communism led him to increase the American involvement in Vietnam that had already begun under Eisenhower. Historian Herbert S. Parmet stated that in Kennedy's decisions regarding "Southeast Asia, in particular, he left behind a prescription for even greater disasters to come."[5] Ultimately, the United States suffered more than fifty thousand casualties there.

In domestic affairs, he failed to get Congress to pass many measures. Kennedy lacked the drive and focus necessary for working with congressional members to get his programs passed. Nevertheless, he broadened welfare, housing, and job training programs. He increased the minimum wage and Social Security. These measures improved the quality of life for many Americans.

John F. Kennedy's most indelible domestic contribution will always be the civil rights movement. Although initially cautious in his support, Kennedy gradually changed his view. He used the power of the presidency to enforce laws already on the books. Historian Parmet praised Kennedy's recognition that the time was right to pursue the cause of civil rights: "When the time came, he [Kennedy] provided the leadership that the struggle for equality had always needed from the White House."[6] At the time of his death, Kennedy was working toward expanded civil rights legislation. The Civil Rights Act of 1964, which was passed during the Johnson administration, was actually part of Kennedy's legacy.

Kennedy lived at a time when the threat of nuclear war seemed very real. Yet he was determined to pursue peace. His June 1963 speech at American University pledging to work toward world peace and to pursue the nuclear test-ban treaty with the USSR and Great Britain contained strong statements for those times.[7] Also, the Peace Corps and the Alliance for Progress built up the image of an America committed to creating a better, more peaceful world. According to Professor Giglio, programs such as the Peace Corps improved the image that newly emerging nations in Asia and Africa held of the United States.[8]

When Kennedy took office, the United States lagged behind the Soviet Union in the space race. However, America put the first man on the moon in 1969, just as Kennedy had promised in 1961. The United States space launch compound in Cape Canaveral, Florida, is now known as the Kennedy Space Center.

With the help of his wife, John F. Kennedy also encouraged the development of culture. After Kennedy's death, President Lyndon Johnson asked Congress to rename the National Cultural Center in Washington, D.C., after Kennedy. Today, the John F. Kennedy Center for the Performing Arts includes six theaters and recognizes all the arts. In addition, Kennedy's fitness program for youth, requiring a minimum standard of fitness for all, contributed to the overall health of the nation.

Although Kennedy spent only one thousand days in office, Americans continue to hold him in high esteem. In a Gallup poll taken in 1983, he was rated the nation's most popular president.[9] Two thirds of those polled believed that the United States would have been "much different" had he lived.[10]

Although Kennedy would undoubtedly have appreciated his high public approval rating, he would probably have been more interested in knowing how historians ranked him. He believed that a president should be rated by his

SOURCE DOCUMENT

An unbelievable tragedy. Let mankind ensure that his beliefs & actions — the cause of freedom & justice are not lost.
David Right, Streams, Kent.
25/11/63.

My deepest sympathy to Mrs. Kennedy, her family and the people of America on the loss of a husband, father and President. Joan Hinchliffe
Romford, Essex 25/11/63.

This cowardly and unprovoked murder of the young and energetic president is base, it brutal it is bad, is beastly and wrong. It is so revolting that I could not comfort myself let alone find words enough find words enough for the bereaved family. Please Jackie accept my heartfelt Sympathy
Uwafili Ofulue 25/11/63.

To Mrs. Kennedy — Your country has lost a great man — but my condolences are to you—his wife. Knowing how complete & private is your grief, & how bereft you feel I extend to you my heartfelt sympathy
Noreen M. Munier (Miss), Ealing, W.5.

The world has lost not only a great and important leader but also a great man who faced his responsibilities to his family and country with unsurpassed courage and humanity. To Mrs Kennedy who has suffered more than any single woman deserves sincere condolences
Steven Carson.
25/11/63

After Kennedy was assassinated, people all over the world came to express their grief in memory books provided by embassies and public buildings. This page is taken from the memory book in the American Embassy in London.

specific achievements.[11] Nearly twenty years after Kennedy's death, one thousand scholars ranked the presidents from George Washington through Jimmy Carter on their effectiveness. Kennedy was rated as an above-average president, and of the nine presidents who served less than one full term, Kennedy is the only one rated higher than average.[12] Still, scholars and historians, in judging both his accomplishments and his failures, chose not to rate him as a great president. This is a less romanticized view of John F. Kennedy than is held by the general public.

Kennedy's casual and youthful leadership style increased Americans' awareness of the need for each citizen to take action. According to Bill Moyers, an aide to Lyndon Johnson, the 1960s were "a time when we believed individuals could demand that government do good and government could ensure individuals the chance to do their best."[13] Kennedy's New Frontier supplied the vision that individual American citizens could make a difference in the world.

It is interesting to contemplate what more the New Frontier might have accomplished if John F. Kennedy had lived to complete his first term. Or would Kennedy's human flaws eventually have ended the myth of Camelot?

Chronology

1917—Born in Brookline, Massachusetts, May 29.

1930—Attended and graduated from the Choate School in
–1935 Wallingford, Connecticut.

1935—Went to London to study economics but returned because of jaundice attack; entered Princeton University that fall; withdrew because of jaundice.

1936—Attended and graduated from Harvard University;
–1940 senior thesis published as *Why England Slept*.

1941—Enlisted in the United States Navy in September.

1943—Given command of PT-109; won Navy and Marine Corps medal for bravery in rescue of PT-109 crew.

1944—Brother Joseph P. Kennedy, Jr., killed in World War II bombing mission.

1945—Wrote articles for Hearst newspapers.

1946—Elected to Congress from Eleventh District of
–1952 Massachusetts; served three terms.

1952—Elected to United States Senate from Massachusetts.

1953—Married Jacqueline Bouvier on September 12.

1954—Underwent back surgery on October 21.

1955—Underwent second back surgery in February; wrote *Profiles in Courage*.

1956—Defeated in bid for vice-presidential nomination at the Democratic National Convention.

1957—Won Pulitzer Prize for *Profiles in Courage*; daughter Caroline born on November 27.

1958—Reelected to United States Senate.

1960—Elected president of the United States; son John F. Kennedy, Jr., born on November 25.

1961—Established Peace Corps and Alliance for Progress; Bay of Pigs invasion; announced space program to put a man on the moon by the end of the 1960s; Berlin Wall crisis; increased American commitment of advisers to South Vietnam.

1962—Steel crisis; enrollment of James Meredith at the University of Mississippi; Cuban Missile Crisis.

1963—Speech on world peace at American University; proposed major civil rights legislation; *"Ich bin ein Berliner"* speech in Berlin; birth of son Patrick Bouvier Kennedy on August 7, death of infant on August 9; Dr. Martin Luther King, Jr.'s march on Washington; signed Nuclear Test-Ban Treaty.

1963—Assassinated in Dallas, Texas, on November 22.

Chapter Notes

Chapter 1. Disaster in Dallas

1. Herbert S. Parmet, *JFK: The Presidency of John F. Kennedy* (New York: The Dial Press, 1983), p. 343.

2. "In Their Own Words," in *The Dallas Morning News, The Day JFK Died* (Kansas City: Andrews and McMeel, 1993), p. 15.

3. Ralph G. Martin, *A Hero for Our Time* (New York: Ballantine Books, 1983), p. 515.

4. "In Their Own Words," p. 16.

5. John H. Davis, *The Kennedys: Dynasty and Disaster* (New York: Shapolsky, 1992), p. 523.

6. Conover Hunt, *JFK For a New Generation* (Dallas: The Sixth Floor Museum and Southern Methodist University Press, 1996), p. 8.

7. Wilborn Hampton, *Kennedy Assassinated! The World Mourns* (Cambridge, Mass.: Candlewick Press, 1997), p. 18.

8. Hunt, p. 36.

Chapter 2. Growing Up a Kennedy

1. Herbert S. Parmet, *Jack: The Struggles of John F. Kennedy* (New York: The Dial Press, 1980), p. 10.

2. Doris Kearns Goodwin, *The Fitzgeralds and the Kennedys* (New York: St. Martin's Press, 1987), p. 339.

3. Nigel Hamilton, *JFK: Reckless Youth* (New York: Random House, Inc., 1992), p. 215.

4. Ibid., p. 85.

5. Thomas C. Reeves, *A Question of Character: A Life of John F. Kennedy* (New York: Free Press, 1997), p. 32.

6. Ibid.

7. Ibid., p. 28.

8. Hamilton, p. 91.

9. Goodwin, p. 427.

10. Hamilton, p. 127.

11. Ibid., pp. 132–133.

12. Reeves, p. 42.

13. Ralph G. Martin, *A Hero for Our Time* (New York: Ballantine Books, 1983), p. 33.

14. Ibid.

Chapter 3. The Coming of War

1. Doris Kearns Goodwin, *The Fitzgeralds and the Kennedys* (New York: St. Martin's Press, 1987), p. 582.

2. Thomas C. Reeves, *A Question of Character: A Life of John F. Kennedy* (New York: Free Press, 1997), pp. 48–49.

3. Ibid., p. 49.

4. Nigel Hamilton, *JFK: Reckless Youth* (New York: Random House, Inc., 1992), p. 388.

5. Ibid., p. 230.

6. Herbert S. Parmet, *Jack: The Struggles of John F. Kennedy* (New York: The Dial Press, 1980), pp. 14–15.

7. Ibid., p. 86.

8. Hank Searls, *The Lost Prince: Young Joe, the Forgotten Kennedy* (New York: World Publishing Co., 1969), p. 174.

9. Robert Bulkeley, *At Close Quarters* (Washington, D.C.: U.S. Government Printing Office, 1962), p. 29.

10. Hamilton, p. 542.

11. Ibid., p. 543.

12. James MacGregor Burns, *John Kennedy: A Political Profile* (New York: Avon Book Division, 1960), p. 62.

13. Hamilton, p. 607.

14. Ibid., p. 108.

15. Goddard Lieberson, ed., *John Fitzgerald Kennedy . . . As We Remember Him* (New York: Atheneum, 1965), p. 45.

16. Reeves, p. 67.

17. Ibid., p. 63; Peter Collier and David Horowitz, *The Kennedys: An American Drama* (New York: Warner Books, Inc., 1984), p. 155.

18. Theodore C. Sorensen, *Kennedy* (New York: Konecky & Konecky, 1965), p. 18.

19. Rose Kennedy, *Times to Remember* (Garden City, N.Y.: Doubleday, 1974), p. 285.

20. Parmet, p. 127.

21. Ibid., p. 126.

22. Joan Blair and Clay Blair, Jr., *The Search for JFK* (New York: Berkley Publishing Corporation, 1976), p. 30.

23. Ralph G. Martin, *A Hero for Our Time* (New York: Ballantine Books, 1983), p. 43.

Chapter 4. Going to Congress

1. Joan Blair and Clay Blair, Jr., *The Search for JFK* (New York: Berkley Publishing Corporation, 1976), p. 356.

2. Herbert S. Parmet, *Jack: The Struggles of John F. Kennedy* (New York: The Dial Press, 1980), pp. 149–150.

3. Doris Kearns Goodwin, *The Fitzgeralds and the Kennedys* (New York: St. Martin's Press, 1987), p. 711.

4. Parmet, p. 155.

5. Thomas C. Reeves, *A Question of Character: A Life of John F. Kennedy* (New York: Free Press, 1997), pp. 87–88.

6. Ibid., p. 86.

7. Blair, p. 516.

8. Ibid., p. 561.

9. Theodore C. Sorensen, *Kennedy* (New York: Konecky & Konecky, 1965), p. 38.

10. Goodwin, p. 745.

11. Parmet, pp. 218–220.

12. Ibid., p. 221.

13. C. David Heymann, *A Woman Named Jackie* (New York: Carol Publishing Group, 1989), p. 106.

Chapter 5. Senator Kennedy

1. Thomas C. Reeves, *A Question of Character: A Life of John F. Kennedy* (New York: Free Press, 1997), p. 98.

2. Herbert S. Parmet, *Jack: The Struggles of John F. Kennedy* (New York: The Dial Press, 1980), p. 236.

3. Reeves, p. 103.

4. Parmet, p. 253.

5. James MacGregor Burns, *John Kennedy: A Political Profile* (New York: Avon Books, 1960), p. 127.

6. Reeves, p. 111.

7. Ralph G. Martin, *A Hero for Our Time* (New York: Ballantine Books, 1983), p. 75.

8. C. David Heymann, *A Woman Named Jackie* (New York: Carol Publishing Group, 1994), p. 120.

9. Martin, p. 77.

10. Ibid., p. 90.

11. Peter Collier and David Horowitz, *The Kennedys: An American Drama* (New York: Warner Books, Inc., 1984), pp. 241–242.

12. Parmet, p. 299.

13. Ibid.

14. Ibid., p. 300; Joan Blair and Clay Blair, Jr., *The Search for JFK* (New York: Berkley Publishing Corporation, 1976), p. 317.

15. Heymann, p. 170.

16. Ibid., p. 171.

17. Parmet, pp. 320–323.

18. Reeves, p. 126.

19. Heymann, p. 180.

20. Reeves, p. 116; Parmet, pp. 296–299.

21. Heymann, pp. 191–192.

22. Richard Reeves, *President Kennedy: Profile of Power* (New York: Simon & Schuster, 1993), p. 15.

23. Martin, p. 113.

24. Doris Kearns Goodwin, *The Fitzgeralds and the Kennedys* (New York: St. Martin's Press, 1987), p. 785.

25. Heymann, p. 192.

26. Ibid., p. 193.

27. Thomas C. Reeves, p. 138.

28. Ibid.

29. Heymann, p. 193.

30. Parmet, p. 389.

31. Goodwin, p. 793.

32. Thomas C. Reeves, p. 146.

Chapter 6. The Road to the Presidency

1. Thomas C. Reeves, *A Question of Character: A Life of John F. Kennedy* (New York: Free Press, 1997), p. 146.

2. Doris Kearns Goodwin, *The Fitzgeralds and the Kennedys* (New York: St. Martin's Press, 1987), p. 798.

3. Ralph G. Martin, *A Hero for Our Time* (New York: Ballantine Books, 1983), p. 203.

4. Herbert S. Parmet, *JFK: The Presidency of John F. Kennedy* (New York: The Dial Press, 1983), p. 23.

5. Ibid., pp. 13, 29.

6. Arthur M. Schlesinger, Jr., *A Thousand Days: John F. Kennedy in the White House* (Boston, Mass.: Houghton Mifflin Company, 1965), p. 47.

7. Carl M. Brauer, "John F. Kennedy," in Henry Graff, ed., *The Presidents: A Reference History* (New York: Charles Scribner's Sons, 1996), p. 484.

8. Parmet, pp. 23, 27.

9. Schlesinger, p. 58.

10. John F. Kennedy, *Let the Word Go Forth* (New York: Delacorte Press, 1988), p. 101.

11. Eric Foner and John A. Garraty, eds., *The Reader's Companion to American History* (Boston, Mass.: Houghton Mifflin Company, 1991), p. 790.

12. Harris Wofford, *Of Kennedys and Kings* (Pittsburgh, Pa.: University of Pittsburgh Press, 1980), p. ix.

13. Reeves, p. 220.

14. Ibid., p. 222.

15. Schlesinger, p. 256.

16. James N. Giglio, *The Presidency of John F. Kennedy* (Lawrence: University of Kansas Press, 1991), p. 21.

Chapter 7. Life in the White House

1. National Archives and Record Administration, *Kennedy's Inaugural Address of 1961* (Washington, D.C.: National Archives Trust Board, 1987), p. 24.

2. Harris Wofford, *Of Kennedys and Kings* (Pittsburgh, Pa.: University of Pittsburgh, 1980), p. 489.

3. Ibid.

4. Ralph G. Martin, *A Hero for Our Time* (New York: Ballantine Books, 1983), p. 248.

5. Arthur M. Schlesinger, Jr., *A Thousand Days: John F. Kennedy in the White House* (New York: Houghton Mifflin Company, 1965), p. 667.

6. Peter Collier and David Horowitz, *The Kennedys: An American Drama* (New York: Warner Books, Inc., 1984), p. 393.

7. Martin, p. 484.

8. Thomas C. Reeves, *A Question of Character: A Life of John F. Kennedy* (New York: Free Press, 1997), pp. 249–250.

9. Herbert S. Parmet, *JFK: The Presidency of John F. Kennedy* (New York: The Dial Press, 1983), p. 86.

10. Reeves, p. 250.

11. Alex Ayers, ed., *The Wit and Wisdom of John F. Kennedy* (New York: Penguin Books, 1996), p. 106.

Chapter 8. Building a New Frontier

1. National Archives and Record Administration, *Kennedy's Inaugural Address of 1961* (Washington, D.C.: National Archives Trust Board, 1987), p. 4.

2. Ibid.

3. Harris Wofford, *Of Kennedys and Kings* (Pittsburgh, Pa.: University of Pittsburgh Press, 1980), p. xi.

4. Ralph G. Martin, *A Hero for Our Time* (New York: Ballantine Books, 1983), p. 303.

5. Arthur M. Schlesinger, Jr., *A Thousand Days* (Boston, Mass.: Houghton Mifflin Company, 1965), pp. 242–243.

6. Alan Brinkley, *American History: A Survey* (New York: McGraw-Hill, Inc., 1995), p. 832.

7. Herbert S. Parmet, *JFK: The Presidency of John F. Kennedy* (New York: The Dial Press, 1983), p. 157.

8. Richard Reeves, *President Kennedy: Profile of Power* (New York: Simon & Schuster, 1993), p. 94.

9. Carl M. Brauer, "John F. Kennedy," in Henry Graff, ed., *The Presidents: A Reference History* (New York: Charles Scribner's Sons, 1996), p. 492.

10. Reeves, p. 101.

11. Parmet, p. 179.

12. Ibid., p. 136.

13. Wofford, p. 489.

14. Schlesinger, pp. 930–931.

15. Peter Collier and David Horowitz, *The Kennedys: An American Drama* (New York: Warner Books, Inc., 1984), p. 344–345.

16. Thomas C. Reeves, *A Question of Character: A Life of John F. Kennedy* (New York: Free Press, 1997), p. 294.

17. C. David Heymann, *A Woman Named Jackie* (New York: Carol Publishing Group, 1994), p. 302.

18. "Berlin," *Microsoft Encarta Encyclopedia*, 1999 Edition.

19. Parmet, p. 197.

20. Thomas C. Reeves, p. 306.

21. Richard Reeves, p. 214.

22. Thomas C. Reeves, p. 313.

23. Collier and Horowitz, p. 362.

24. Thomas C. Reeves, p. 314.

Chapter 9. Challenges and Successes

1. Thomas C. Reeves, *A Question of Character: A Life of John F. Kennedy* (New York: Free Press, 1997), p. 290.

2. Richard Reeves, *President Kennedy: Profile of Power* (New York: Simon & Schuster, 1993), p. 295.

3. John F. Kennedy, *Let the Word Go Forth* (New York: Delacort Press, 1988), p. 159.

4. Herbert S. Parmet, *JFK: The Presidency of John F. Kennedy* (New York: The Dial Press, 1983), p. 206.

5. Ibid., p. 260.

6. Richard Reeves, p. 364.

7. Ibid., p. 379.

8. James N. Giglio, *The Presidency of John F. Kennedy* (Lawrence: University of Kansas Press, 1991), p. 198.

9. Arthur M. Schlesinger, Jr., *A Thousand Days: John F. Kennedy in the White House* (New York: Houghton Mifflin Company, 1965), p. 805.

10. National Archives and Records Administration, *The Cuban Missile Crisis* (Washington, D.C.: National Archives Trust Fund Board, 1988), p. 4.

11. Schlesinger, p. 812.

12. Robert F. Kennedy, *Thirteen Days* (New York: W. W. Norton & Company, Inc., 1969), p. 54.

13. John F. Kennedy, p. 275.

14. National Archives, p. 29.

15. Ibid., p. 9.

16. Parmet, p. 292.

17. Giglio, p. 206.

18. Schlesinger, p. 818.

19. Giglio, p. 208.

20. Robert F. Kennedy, p. 82.

21. Giglio, pp. 210–211.

22. Schlesinger, p. 829.

23. Ralph G. Martin, *A Hero for Our Time* (New York: Ballantine Books, 1983), p. 424.

24. Thomas C. Reeves, p. 394.

25. Martin, p. 476.

26. Richard Reeves, p. 515.

27. John F. Kennedy, p. 327.

28. Ibid., p. 328.

29. Thomas C. Reeves, p. 400.

30. C. David Heymann, *A Woman Named Jackie* (New York: Carol Publishing Group, 1994), p. 418.

31. Giglio, p. 186.

32. Richard Reeves, p. 643.

33. Edwin O. Guthman and Jeffrey Shulman, *Robert Kennedy: In His Own Words* (New York: Bantam Books, 1988), p. 394.

34. Parmet, pp. 328, 336.

Chapter 10. Assassination Aftermath

1. "In Their Own Words," in *The Dallas Morning News, The Day JFK Died* (Kansas City: Andrews and McMeel, 1993), p. 50.

2. Mark Lane, *Rush to Judgment* (New York: Thunder's Mouth Press, 1966), pp. 8, 12.

3. Ibid., p. 69; Harrison Edward Livingstone, *High Treason 2* (New York: Carroll & Graf Publishers, Inc., 1992), pp. 73–74, 565.

4. Conover Hunt, *JFK for a New Generation* (Dallas: The Sixth Floor Museum and Southern Methodist University Press, 1996), p. 75.

5. Kent Biffle, "John Connally," in *The Dallas Morning News, The Day JFK Died* (Kansas City: Andrews and McMeel, 1993), p. 100.

6. Lane, p. 71.

7. Lane, p. 127.

8. Hunt, p. 74.

9. James H. Fetzer, ed., *Assassination Science* (Chicago, Ill.: Catfeet Press, 1998), p. 136.

10. Jeffrey Waggoner, *The Assassination of President Kennedy* (San Diego, Calif.: Greenhaven Press, Inc., 1989), p. 103.

11. Fetzer, p. 358; David Lifton, *Best Evidence* (New York: Macmillan, 1980), p. 506.

12. Waggoner, p. 103.

13. Fetzer, pp. 37, 49–50; Lifton, pp. 55–69; Mark Lane, *Plausible Denial* (New York: Thunder's Mouth Press, 1991), p. 17.

14. Lane, p. 51.

15. Fetzer, pp. 37, 57.

16. Lane, p. 51.

17. Jim Marrs, *Crossfire: The Plot That Killed Kennedy* (New York: Carroll & Graf, Publishers, Inc., 1989), pp. 56–60.

18. Hunt, p. 79.

19. Jim Garrison, *On the Trail of the Assassins* (New York: Sheridan Square Press, 1988), p. 276.

20. Oliver Stone and Zachary Sklar, with Jane Rusconi, *JFK: The Book of the Film* (Santa Barbara, Calif.: Applause Books, 1992), p. 199.

21. Hunt, p. 111.

22. Garrison, pp. xi–xii.

23. Ibid., p 277.

24. Bill Deemer, "Enduring Questions: Conspiracy Theories Persist," in *The Dallas Morning News*, p. 107.

Chapter 11. Legacy

1. Harris Wofford, *Of Kennedys and Kings* (Pittsburgh, Pa.: University of Pittsburgh Press, 1980), p. 36.

2. James N. Giglio, *The Presidency of John F. Kennedy* (Lawrence: University of Kansas Press, 1991), p. 285.

3. Thomas C. Reeves, *A Question of Character* (New York: Simon & Schuster, 1997), p. 417.

4. Ibid., pp. 264–265, 276.

5. Herbert S. Parmet, *JFK: The Presidency of John F. Kennedy* (New York: The Dial Press, 1983), pp. 352–353.

6. Ibid., p. 354.

7. Ibid.

8. Giglio, p. 285.

9. Ibid., p. 282.

10. Ibid.

11. Ibid., p. 283.

12. Robert K. Murray and Tim H. Blessing, *Greatness in the White House: Rating the Presidents, Washington through Carter* (University Park: Pennsylvania State University Press, 1988), p. 16.

13. Wofford, p. x.

Further Reading

Gow, Catherine. *The Cuban Missile Crisis*. San Diego, Calif.: Lucent Books, 1997.

Graves, Charles P. *John F. Kennedy: New Frontiersman*. New York: Chelsea House, 1992.

Hampton, Wilborn. *Kennedy Assassinated! The World Mourns: A Reporter's Story*. Cambridge, Mass.: Candlewick Press, 1997.

Hunt, Conover. *JFK for a New Generation*. Dallas: The Sixth Floor Museum and Southern Methodist University Press, 1996.

Netzley, Patricia D. *The Assassination of President John F. Kennedy*. New York: New Discovery Books, 1994.

Pietrusza, David. *John F. Kennedy*. San Diego, Calif.: Lucent Books, 1997.

The President's Commission on the Assassination of President John F. Kennedy. *The Warren Report: The Report of the President's Commission on the Assassination of President John F. Kennedy*. Washington, D.C.: Associated Press, 1964.

Schuman, Michael. *Lyndon B. Johnson*. Springfield, N.J.: Enslow Publishers, Inc., 1998.

———. *Richard M. Nixon*. Springfield, N.J.: Enslow Publishers, Inc., 1998.

United States House of Representatives. *The Final Assassinations Report: Report of the Select Committee on Assassinations*. New York: Bantam Books, 1979.

Waggoner, Jeffrey. *The Assassination of President Kennedy*. San Diego, Calif.: Greenhaven Press, Inc., 1989.

Places to Visit

Florida

Kennedy Space Center Visitor Complex, Cape Canaveral. (407) 452-2121. The center is the site for all United States space launches. A limited number of car passes are available to watch launches from the NASA Causeway at the center. Models of the lunar rover, space suits, and other space memorabilia are on display. Open daily at 9 A.M. except for December 25. Closing hours vary from 7 to 9 P.M., depending on launch schedule and amount of daylight.

Massachusetts

John F. Kennedy Library and Museum, Columbia Point. (617) 929-4500. Twenty-five exhibits use film and television footage, presidential documents, and family keepsakes to portray Kennedy's years growing up and his time as president. Open daily from 9 A.M. to 5 P.M. except January 1, Thanksgiving, and December 25.

John Fitzgerald Kennedy National Historic Site, Brookline. (617) 566-7937. The site preserves the nine-room home in which Kennedy was born. Displayed are photos and mementos of the president collected by his mother. Open Wednesday–Sunday, mid-March through November, from 10:00 A.M. to 4:30 P.M. except for major holidays.

Texas

The Sixth Floor Museum at Dealey Plaza, Dallas. (214) 747-6660. The museum is located on the sixth floor of the former Texas School Book Depository. Two blocks away is the John

F. Kennedy Memorial, a cenotaph, or open tomb. Exhibits describe Kennedy's presidency, his fateful trip to Dallas, and the two official government investigations of his death. The museum is open daily except Thanksgiving and Christmas from 9 A.M. to 6 P.M.

Washington, D.C.

John F. Kennedy Center for the Performing Arts. (202) 416-8341. Kennedy played a leadership role in raising funds for the center, which was originally known as the National Cultural Center. Congress voted to change the name two months after Kennedy's death. In six theaters plays, musicals, ballets, concerts, children's theater and other events are performed. Open daily from 10 A.M. to 9 P.M. except for January 1 and December 25. Tours from 10 A.M. to 1 P.M.

Internet Addresses

The American Experience: The Presidents
<http://www.pbs.org/wgbh/pages/amex/presidents/ nf/featured/featured.html>

The Cuban Missile Crisis
<http://www.encarta.msn.com/explore/yearbook/ archive/mar98/cuban/ybb_max3.as>

The History Channel—Great Speeches:
Hear the Words That Changed the World
<http://www.historychannel.com/gspeech/ archive.html>

The History Place: JFK Photo History
<http://www.historyplace.com/kennedy/ gallery.htm>

Inaugural Addresses of the Presidents of the United States
<http://www.columbia.edu/acis/bartleby/inaugural/index.html>

In Their Own Words
<http://www.pbs.org/wgbh/pages/amex/presidents/nf/words/words.html>

John Fitzgerald Kennedy
<http://www.randolph.pvt.k12.al.us/homepage/msmulti/osland/credits.html>

The John F. Kennedy Center for the Performing Arts
<http://kennedy-center.org>

John F. Kennedy Library and Museum
<http://www.cs.umb.edu/jfk/index/htm>

John Fitzgerald Kennedy National Historic Site
<http://www.nps.gov/jofi>

Kennedy Space Center
<http://www.ksc.nasa.gov/ksc.html>

President John F. Kennedy Assassination Records Collection Reference System (National Archives, College Park, Maryland)
<http://www.nara.gov/nara/jfk/jfk_search.html>

The Sixth Floor Museum at Dealey Plaza
<http://www.jfk.org>

Index